M000316029

remembering
1969

remembering 1969

Searching for the Eternal in Changing Times

An Allegorical Memoir
by Robert Atkinson

Bahá'í
PUBLISHING
Wilmette, Illinois

Bahá'í Publishing
415 Linden Avenue, Wilmette, Illinois 60091-2844
Copyright © 2008 by the National Spiritual Assembly of the Bahá'ís of
the United States
All rights reserved. Published 2008
Printed in the United States of America on acid-free paper ∞

11   10   09   08   4   3   2   1

Library of Congress Cataloging-in-Publication Data
Atkinson, Robert, Ph. D.
   Remembering 1969 : searching for the eternal in changing times / by
Robert Atkinson.
      p. cm.
   Includes bibliographical references.
   ISBN-13: 978-1-931847-54-4
   ISBN-10: 1-931847-54-1
   1. Atkinson, Robert, Ph. D. 2. Spiritual biography. I. Title.

BL73.A85A3 2008
297.9'3092—dc22
[B]
                                                            2007041595

Lyrics from the following songs are quoted herein by permission:

Gabriel's Mother's Highway Ballad #16 Blues
by Arlo Guthrie
© Copyright 1970 (Renewed) by Howard Beach Music, Inc.
All Rights reserved. Used by Permission.

Highway in the Wind
by Arlo Guthrie
© Copyright 1967 (Renewed) by APPLESEED MUSIC, INC.
All Rights Reserved. Used by Permission.

Time and Love
Words and Music by Laura Nyro
© 1966 (Renewed 1994) EMI BLACKWOOD MUSIC INC.
All Rights Reserved. International Copyright Secured. Used by Permission.

The Balance
Words and Music by Graeme Edge and Ray Thomas
© 1970 (Renewed 1998) GYMHOUSE LTD. and MEMFOREST LTD.
All Rights Controlled and Administered by COLGEMS-EMI MUSIC INC.
All Rights Reserved. International Copyright Secured. Used by Permission.

Cover photo printed with permission of Hudson River Sloop Clearwater, Inc.,
photo by Steve Stanne.
Cover and book design by Suni D. Hannan.

For my parents and grandparents

"For the son who has grown really to know the father,
the agonies of the ordeal are readily borne;
the world is no longer a vale of tears
but a bliss-yielding, perpetual manifestation of the Presence."
—Joseph Campbell, *The Hero with a Thousand Faces*

Contents

Foreword

There is a new kind of sacred literature emerging into the collective mindscape. It does not follow the canons or articles of faith of any known tradition, religious—or literary for that matter—but rather emerges out of a contemporary life, lived under the open skies of metaphysical exploration. In this emergent genre, the individual finds his/her way to a personal gnosis, a unique biographical penetration of the mystery of life—and a nugget, a personal gem of wisdom is extracted. It is usually both personal and transpersonal—a paradox. If the encounter with experience is done with integrity, there is a flowing forth of wisdom from a transcendent Source—something is touched in our own experience of living, and it may be shared with others.

Robert Atkinson's memoir begins in an early life—as a sensitive boy struggles with a flaw—a speech impediment. His voice lacks inner authority it seems—and thus a quest is initiated. He begins listening to a voiceless voice that speaks within his own soul—guiding him. He takes the advice and finds himself on a timeless adventure. As Joseph Campbell said, "If you follow your bliss, doors will open for you that you didn't even know were there."

Bob Atkinson finds himself sniffing down the corridors of the possible—synchronicities begin to unfold all around him—and he realizes he is in a subtle game of discovery with the materials of his life. His period of becoming is well synchronized to that of a generation engaged in a creative re-thinking of the world . . . the sixties, magic times, magic places.

Atkinson's daimon leads him to the launching of the ship *Clearwater,* a noble experiment in the dawning of a new consciousness, in which environmentalism, humanism, and a new spirituality seem to be breaking simultaneously into the mindscape of the culture. The *Clearwater* was destined to become famous—the heart of local festivals up and down the Hudson River, and the inauguration of a focal movement toward clean water and air. (It is important to realize just how influential that time and those events were, as we now enjoy a scenic Hudson one can swim and fish in—and the *Clearwater* still plies the river, spreading joy, raising ecological awareness.)

Atkinson's contact with Pete Seeger and Arlo Guthrie, and the galaxy of talented visionaries around them, lends a mythic air to the landscape of the Hudson Valley—an epiphany seems to hide behind every rock, and in every glade; and the local myth of Rip van Winkle, the ever-awakening man, becomes a parable of the awakening human soul.

Atkinson lives first like an anchorite-mystic in a rustic cabin in the woods, then takes lodging in a monastery to weather out the New York winter. It seems a place of genuine wisdom and charity, where the homeless are succored. Here through dream and vision, our hero finally seems to come into his own as a spiritual pilgrim, walking his path with new devotion and strength. His insights are not unfamiliar to students of the Perennial Philosophy; the path is based on the cultivation of love—and a faith in the guidance that keeps surprising us with its appropriateness. As the journey becomes decidedly more mythic, Atkinson meets an appropriate guide—Campbell himself—through a surprising series of synchronicities.

Joseph Campbell did for Robert Atkinson what he did for many a young writer or creative artist: set him firmly on the path to himself. Not through directing him, this way or that, but by pointing to the landmarks that have been left by human heroes on their parallel paths since time out of mind. "Peace, traveler, only look at the signs around you, and follow the burning in your own heart. Then your feet will not stray."

The denouement of this lovely story of one man's journey to selfhood comes through another synchronicity whereby he is hired by his own alma mater to teach a course in the life-wisdom transmitted by the lyrics of folk and popular music. A more apt invitation could not have been found in the light of Atkinson's recent journey. Now his speech impediment is overcome, not because he has strengthened his vocal cords, but because he has tempered his soul. The authentic voice begins to emerge effortlessly, and what it speaks is soul-lore. Thus the transpersonal and the personal are woven together, and Atkinson realizes the import of Campbell's parting words to him: "The archetypes of your experience represent your most reliable truth.

Integrate them into your daily living. Transmit their meaning to others."

This indeed is what Professor Robert Atkinson has done in his career since the extraordinary life-transformative period that forms the main substance of this beautiful little book. Teach fearlessly out of his own authentic experience—and with an essential voice. Listen to it, and you will find it full of wisdom and poetry—and an empowerment of your own mythic journey.

Stephen Larsen
New Paltz, New York

Preface

Writing a memoir is inherently presumptuous. But, like giving birth after conception, at some point the process takes over. Originally, the heart of what you see here came forth in 1971 as an epic poem after I sensed the completion of a series of serendipitous adventures, a two-year cycle compressed here into four seasons. I couldn't help then but put these experiences and my thoughts around them in writing, if only for my own benefit. That creative effort did need to be fleshed out, obviously, which led to numerous drafts and revisions. None of them, apparently, were ready for anyone else but me, until now.

In the many years since the birth of this memoir, much has become clearer to me about this part of my life. My understanding of my own experience has taken on greater and greater meaning because I have reflected deeply upon it for many years. But this is a never-ending process. I am still amazed at, and humbled by, all that happened then, and how everything that did happen seems to be exactly what was needed in my life.

I only gradually began to feel comfortable in considering that this might be read by others. It has taken me this long to be okay with however my actions might be compared to my written words. But my greatest realization in needing to put my experience down in words, going over them endlessly, and trying to make them always clearer, is that these things that happened *to* me are archetypal experiences that are meant to connect us to each other.

In some mysterious way, my experience is more than just mine. This time in my life represents the convergence of critical moments in personal, historical, and cultural time. It is the most profound of transitional moments, a time of inner preparation, a time of maturing into roles yet to be defined. I tell my story that you may see in it something of your own story.

This has ultimately made the telling of my story even more challenging. I have consciously chosen to emphasize my internal understandings of the unique circumstances of my life, and their meanings for me, rather than fully develop the concreteness of the external events themselves that helped facilitate these understandings.

In so doing, I hope to more closely approach the universal in all our stories. The title I have chosen for this memoir is meant to highlight a few key events of a particular time that many were changed by, but to really put the focus on what lies beyond change.

I ask only, as might Walt Whitman or Carl Jung, my models of autobiographical reflection, that you suspend your expectation of what a memoir is, of where the details and texture should be, so that you may be able to follow where my reflections took me.

An allegorical memoir, by nature and definition, shifts the focus from the external happenings themselves to the internal interpretations of what they mean. What I have to say about this transformative time in my life is for me best expressed as something other than what was in plain sight. Understanding the significance of what was hidden within the events, and seeking to lift up this essence, has made the writing and rewriting of my story for so long a labor I have gladly borne.

I would like to express my gratitude to my grandparents, my parents, and all the friends I met along the way, especially Richard Orton, Pete and Toshi Seeger, Jack Elliott, Gordon Bok, Don McLean, Allan Aunapu, Judy Kossin, Arlo and Jackie Guthrie, Eric and Emily Knud-Hansen, Joseph Campbell, Father Jeremiah, Brother Joe, Brother Joachim, and Dr. Robert Cooke. I would also like to thank those who have taken the time to read and comment on my story at various points in its evolution: Stanwood Cobb, Marzieh Gail, Bahiyyih Nakhjavani, Anne Gordon, Beverly Jennison, Cynthia Atkinson, Stephen Larsen, Ellen Kleiner, Stephany Evans, Christina Baldwin, Michael Parkin, Kathy Krug, Jennifer Meader, Michael Brady, and especially Terry Cassiday, for her commitment to this project, and Alex McGee, for his superb editorial skills.

remembering
1969

Prologue

I am an only child. Yet like every child, something within me yearns for union. Parades of celebration filled the streets soon after I was born, my mother told me. Not for me, but for the end of one era and the beginning of another. This was when the first atomic bomb turned a world at war into a nuclear village. But peace was elusive, and without realizing, my life became a quest to find it.

It was much later, when ageless archetypes began to emerge from deep within me, that I gradually became aware of the story my life was telling. This is when I realized that my story is much like many others. I shall explain.

I grew up near the potato fields, woods, and waters of eastern Long Island, in the middle ground between my mother (outgoing, responsive, imaginative, and persistent) and my father (quiet, gentle, practical, and easygoing). Living within this dialectic has for me been both a challenge and an opportunity.

When I was three, we moved to a new one-story home in a neighborhood off Main Street in a small farming community with its share of ethnic neighborhoods, from which I would find many of my friends.

My mom and I spent much of our time at home while my dad worked for the state department of agriculture. She was the one who very early set me on a spiritual path—one I am still on today—by reading children's Bible stories to me.

My dad worked around the house when he was not at the office. He kept the lawn and yard in top shape, and inside helped finish a game room in the basement and my bedroom in the attic.

I remember walking down our block to Main Street when I was five or six. I'd try to time it so I'd get to the corner where the noon whistle blew just as my dad drove by on his way home for lunch. He would always stop and give me a ride back. I looked forward to these outings; they gave me a wonderful feeling, a little freedom at one end, a lot of security at the other.

My dad and I did many things together, mostly sports. We played catch often, and he was the manager of my Little League team. Because he was always there for me, I felt loved.

My parents provided me with everything I needed and more, but the one thing I had to find on my own was my voice, which turned out to be a long and painful process. I didn't know why, but I was slow to speak. Around the age of three, I began to stutter.

Once I started school, the stuttering increased. It was frustrating and embarrassing. Sometimes, perhaps most of the time, I could speak fine. But on other occasions, I would do everything possible to avoid the pain of being unable to express myself.

There were certain words and sounds I could not articulate—it was as though they were blocked within me. I would take time to think of other words I could say in their place. Sometimes this worked; other times I got stuck. The word I wanted just wouldn't come. I could hear myself say it in my mind, but I would stammer, trying my hardest to get it out, only to end up stuttering my way through it. In time I opted for silence and let my voice go unheard.

My parents were concerned and supportive. They spoke to my teachers. They consulted doctors. But there was nothing anyone could do to prevent the stuttering. Not even my kindergarten teacher, a great ally, could lessen the impact the embarrassment had on me.

I wondered why my voice was trapped within me. Something mysterious kept me from saying all that I could think.

This challenge went on until I was about nine. Then, gradually, my stuttering began to let up. Over the years, it became less noticeable to others, but I continue to carry its effects with me.

Long after I could speak more comfortably, I remained quiet and often stayed in the background. Looking back on what it was like for me in high school, it now seems as if I were sleepwalking through most of it. Even though I had many friends and participated in sports and other events, an important part of me remained dormant, unexpressed.

Everyone has their own burden, their own challenge in life that is unique to them. Childhood stuttering, and how

I viewed my world because of it, has been my struggle. Though clearly not as severe or dramatic as obstacles faced by some, this presented enough of a hurdle for me that it propelled me down a path of self-discovery long before I was aware of it.

When my grandmother came to live with us for several months each year after my grandfather died, around the time I was nine, my stuttering seemed to lessen. Perhaps this timing was more than a coincidence.

I had been intrigued by both my grandparents for some time. My grandfather was an individualistic, freethinking dentist; my grandmother was a gentle, quiet woman, committed to her spiritual life. Their thoughtfulness and love of truth captured my attention early.

My parents, educated only through high school, seemed wise beyond their learning; my grandparents, with their unquenchable desire for knowledge, became models of life-long learning for me.

When my grandmother was with us, she modeled for me the life of the spirit. I observed her often, reading silently from the Bible and *The Upper Room*. Her daily practice of devotion was something new to me then. Yet I must have sensed that the ageless verities were a source of nourishment to her thirsty soul, bringing her closer to God, for I saw clearly that she led a life of gratitude. She spent a good deal of her time doing what she cared most about, and she acted upon her convictions every day with gentle kindness. Her soft words carried the power of a tender, loving spirit.

I don't think I knew it then, but her resolve, her sense of direction, her assurance, and her commitment made a difference to my soul, too. Her quietude and steadfastness invited the extraordinary into her life, and quite possibly into mine as well.

My grandmother lived what my soul yearned for. Her actions planted the seed of hope within me, showing me in her direct but subtle way that I could rely on the signs that came my way, that there was nothing to fear, and, best of all, that I could listen to myself. She also kept alive my wonder, kindling my curiosity for things seen and unseen, and awakening within me a reverence for the mysteries of life.

One day while she was with us, I was sitting on my bed looking out the window, and a "voice" came to me. I could not tell if it was speaking from within me or from somewhere else. The "voice" said, "Someday *you* will know God."

Although I did not understand the meaning of these words, I did begin to get a sense at that moment that this "voice" had something in store for me. It felt like an early warning for something I needed to be on the lookout for.

Many years later, after high school, college, and a year of graduate school, I finally heard from that voice again, during the summer of my twenty-fourth year. I was drawn to people, elders especially, whom I felt had personal wisdom to share about life.

I followed my desire to learn how and why people like my grandmother lived their lives the way they did. While studying folklore in graduate school, I conducted a life story interview with a traditional farmer-singer from the Catskill Mountains. Listening intently to his voice, I began to understand his life as he understood it himself. This allowed me even more of a glimpse of how I wanted my story to unfold.

Then, one day, my life took a turn I had not anticipated. Without much warning, I lost a relationship I thought would last forever. I was alone, discouraged and anxious. The best I could do was turn my gaze inward, seek a deeper meaning in my life, and try to find my inner voice.

I had listened to the voices of others long enough. They had much to tell me, but this was my opportunity to consciously search for where I wanted to be, what I wanted to do, and not settle for where others thought I should fit in the world.

My quest to find my own middle ground—where body, mind, and spirit would merge as one—began when hearing and speaking with my *own* voice became foremost.

This is my story; it is not a history, or a scientific recounting, but the story of my heart. It is a story of the truth that came forth from within me after having lived deeply through a time of great change, a time in my life when only these things I am about to tell you mattered.

I have looked at my life not as a photographer, but with the perspective of a painter rendering a self-portrait. The images that appear here are more as they would appear on a canvas than in a photograph.

This is my personal myth; an allegorical memoir of the adventure of a lifetime. Maybe it will seem familiar to you, too.

Summer

It was July 20, 1969, a day of promise. An early morning mist adorned the swaying dune grass. A breeze stirred; a sparrow sang its gentle song; a golden light rose slowly over the ocean.

The sea foam rolled in along the edge of my fish-shaped isle and dissolved over my toes as I tried to rub from my eyes the remnants of the night. And I thought, "Each step I take this day promises to soothe the shortcomings of yesterday."

CALL

For the first time in my twenty-four years, I had an entire day filled with thought, reflection, and questions. It felt as if a long-dormant part of me was beginning to awaken. Never before had I been so wrapped in meditation.

I was a counselor at a summer camp where I had been drawn by the expectation of a meaningful experience. There I became friends with the head counselor, Richard, who had come to the camp for similar reasons. We soon discovered that we had much in common and decided to try to implement a Summerhill-inspired approach to carrying out activities at the camp. We would not steer the campers toward desired results every moment, but instead would encourage and support them so they could learn to make decisions for themselves.

We believed that a democratic approach would contribute to their thriving and might eventually make them better prepared to assume adult responsibilities. We made it our responsibility to ensure that the campers would have an equal say in how things were run and what activities were planned for them. Richard and I wanted to be there with them and for them, guiding their efforts at community building. Though the camp director's stated purpose was to challenge and inspire the campers, we were repeatedly thwarted in fulfilling this goal because his actions were in direct opposition to it.

Richard's every attempt to carry out the campers' reasonable requests were met with increased resistance by the director. We were frustrated, the campers were growing upset and angry, and the experience was growing less camper-centered by the hour.

About midway through the camp session, during a break after dinner that glorious day, I was out walking along the nearby shoreline. It seemed as though something had to—and was about to—give. I began to anticipate what might be next.

I was filled with excitement when the inner voice I had not heard for years spoke:

Awaken and become conscious of that part of yourself that is part of everyone. Allow yourself to pass beyond the gate of limits into a land of wonder where boundaries cease to exist.

Listen every day as if each sound was just for you to understand. Feel the life in each moment as it comes to you.

Immediately I sensed that something more meaningful than I had known before was possible, even imminent.

When I returned to camp, the other counselors and the campers were all gathered around a television set in the dining hall. The feeling in the room was electric, as if something else of consequence was about to happen.

My thoughts still floating above the shoreline, it was a few moments before I could focus on the image I saw on the television screen. Slowly, a broad panorama of a barren land-scape took shape. The surface appeared soft and grayish, with small craters scattered about.

The picture faded out, then a light appeared and slowly grew larger. The strange landscape again came into view. This time, a thin metal rod pierced the soft surface. As the camera pulled back, I could see that the rod was the leg of a space module. In a flash, its three other legs appeared.

Then came the first sign of movement. A figure in a bulky suit and thick boots began to climb backward, slowly and cautiously, down a nine-rung ladder. One booted foot touched down, silently displacing a flurry of powdery dust. With the second foot on the surface, the figure then began to move about as if learning to walk.

Soon, a second heavily suited figure joined in. Together they glided about, setting all sorts of equipment in place. Before long, one gave the loose powder a playful kick.

They began to bounce around, hopping across the moon's surface like children of the universe. The words coming from the television set penetrated my mind: "One small step for a man, one giant leap for mankind."

As the camera pulled back and shifted direction, there in the distance was the earthrise, a vision of pure beauty, the entire planet as one—strong, yet fragile. This picture struck me as the most compelling photographic image imaginable.

It was the first time I had really seen the earth without boundaries. It occurred to me that the planet is our sanc-tuary, and each and every one of us on it makes up its collective conscience. In this vision, with nothing to di-vide us, the earth appeared as one country. And with billions of individual minds thinking a diversity of thoughts in every corner of this shimmering globe, it became apparent that all of humanity shared a common destiny.

This day *was* different from all others. In seeing our earth from space, I began to see myself differently. How could I find my place within this larger whole? At the same time, I could feel my consciousness shift from the part to the whole and expand to a breadth I had never before fully considered.

As I sat with our little community, I wondered if anyone else was seeing this the way I was. It was too soon to know, but it seemed like there was a deeper significance to this "giant leap for mankind." Could our new vision of the earth be as much a spiritual leap as a technological leap?

How much more are the possibilities for the future now also expanded? Will this great adventure bring us into a new relationship with one another and our universe? How can we not realize that we are all tied together?

Too many questions for one moment, yet I was infused with a sense of hope that these things would come to pass. Capping a decade of deep change, I could even begin to sense this hope in the reaction of the campers.

When the television was turned off, the campers asked if they could stay up a little later to discuss what they had just seen. Richard and I supported them and were quickly impressed with their insightful reactions to the significance of what they had just experienced. But no sooner had they begun than the director characteristically put a stop to this endeavor.

It suddenly seemed like our experiment with equality and self-determination with the campers was nearing its end. We felt frustrated and defeated in achieving our goal at the camp, yet satisfied that we had tried our best given our circumstances.

Later that evening, after the campers had all gone to bed, I went out to the dock to reflect further. With my legs dangling, I sat looking at a sea of stars, the reverse perspective of the image we had just seen up close on the television screen. The moon, in its cycles, seemed to reflect the cycle of my own life, maybe even all life, with its ebb and flow, fullness and emptiness, and repetition of these opposites.

Reflecting further, I first remembered what I was missing across the Sound at the Newport Folk Festival. On this same day I could have seen Pete Seeger, Arlo Guthrie, Joni Mitchell, James Taylor, Johnny Cash, Richie Havens, and others—many long-time, and some new torch-bearers for the folk revival, all songwriters speaking for a generation.

It had been exactly two years previous at Newport that Arlo Guthrie had first sung his meandering tune that was not so much about a restaurant he liked as about a war that he disliked. I recognized that he and the others like him were carrying on a tradition for my generation. There are still many strong voices today, serving as extensions from his father, Woody, and from Pete Seeger, the Weavers, Joe Hill, and others who had previously been voices for social justice in their own generations.

Then it really sunk in. The moonwalk removed barriers for us all. Our new view of the world as a whole gave us a different perspective on what was possible after a long and tumultuous decade.

At that moment, bits of unedited, still-raw memories from the '60s came pouring back, year by year, through my mind. . . .

๛ ๛ ๛

The year 1960 was my first year of high school, when everything in my little corner of the distant and disparate world began to seem much closer, as if the world were getting smaller. Television had made its way into almost every home in the country, bringing images into our living rooms that changed our views of the world we lived in: both rural and urban poverty became more evident, global threats of nuclear weapons became more real from far and near, and domestic signs of racism, a social disease still much worse than we imagined or were able to admit, were coming from every corner.

I was interested in folk music and doo-wop, but out of a long and deep drumming tradition from Africa a totally new global sound, an album called *Drums of Passion*, by Baba Olatunji, caught my attention. Along with the first black student sit-ins in North Carolina that same year, this and other events helped transform a nascent civil rights struggle into a full-fledged national movement, shifting the thinking and values of many white Americans in the process.

Raising our hopes even more, the election of John F. Kennedy promised to bring an end to a painful era of segregation, while his vow to keep us ahead in the space race and to wield a firm hand in the Cold War appealed to just enough people to change the entire atmosphere of the country—maybe even the world—at the outset of the decade.

Two months after his inauguration, President Kennedy established the Peace Corps to promote world peace, friendship, and better understanding among the peoples of the world. I thought at the time, "What better way to really learn about and appreciate differences than by working side by side with others?"

The following month, not long after Fidel Castro began his Communist rule in Cuba, an ill-fated attempt at the Bay of Pigs to remove him raised questions about the president's leadership and turned into the first of many political and social crises of the decade.

A month later, President Kennedy announced his goal of landing a man on the moon before the end of the decade.

The accomplishment of this goal, with only a few months to spare, already felt like it had gone well beyond its intended purpose. The image sent back to the world from the moon has altered our consciousness forever. The lines of separation that appear on all maps are absent on this true-to-life image of the earth; the entire orb appears as one homeland. I wondered if this could lead to the widespread awareness of our organic oneness, and if this could have happened as effectively and on such a large scale in any other way.

My thoughts took me back to 1961, when, a couple of months after Kennedy's vision of space travel was first expressed, things seemed to go in a different direction as another wall of separation went up, between families and relatives, this time dividing the city of Berlin.

Then, the threat of nuclear weapons led to ban-the-bomb protests worldwide. By October of that year, we were warned of possible nuclear attack and advised to build home bomb shelters.

Before his first year in office ended, President Kennedy, at the urging of Eleanor Roosevelt, established the Commission on the Status of Women to look into the progress of women and make recommendations for action—this coming 116 years after Margaret Fuller had written eloquently for complete gender equality:

We would have every arbitrary barrier thrown down. We would have every path laid open to Woman as freely as to Man. Were this done . . . we believe . . . that no discordant collision, but a ravishing harmony of the spheres, would ensue. Yet, then and only then will mankind be ripe for this, when inward and outward freedom for Woman as much as for Man shall be acknowledged as a right, not yielded as a concession.

1962 was marked by nuclear attack threats that upended our daily lives with frequent civil defense drills. When the stare-down over the missiles in Cuba finally ended with their removal and an agreement that we would not attack Cuba, only then did we realize how close the world had come to nuclear annihilation.

At the same time, President Kennedy ordered Governor Wallace to admit black students to the University of Alabama; meanwhile in Mississippi, James Meredith was blocked from attending the university until federal marshals were sent in. The ensuing riots resulted in the tragedy that Bob Dylan sang about in "Oxford Town." He raised the questions that needed to be asked: who is really responsible for these senseless deaths?

What can be done, I thought, to bring back a balance in this endless battle between progress and regress? But in one way or another time always seems to move onward.

In 1963 the balance was readdressed with the publication of Betty Friedan's best-selling *The Feminine Mystique*, signaling the beginning of the end of the idea that women were less than equal to men. The full role of women in society and the extent of their fulfillment were acknowledged and acted upon by women, yet only gradually understood by men. This idea, whose time had clearly arrived, would take its own time to become a social reality.

The summer of 1963, between my high school graduation and the beginning of college, Dr. Martin Luther King Jr., at the massive Civil Rights March on Washington, spoke eloquently and powerfully about his dream of a land united across colors and differences. He reminded everyone, one hundred years after the Emancipation Proclamation, that "the negro still lives on a lonely island of poverty in the midst of a vast ocean of material prosperity." But, he added, "We refuse to believe that the bank of justice is bankrupt. We refuse to believe that there are insufficient funds in the great vaults of opportunity of this nation."

His hope was that this land would be "transformed into an oasis of freedom and justice," and "the jangling discords of our nation into a beautiful symphony of brotherhood." Once again, a Bob Dylan song raised the fitting question: How many times can we turn our heads, pretending we just don't see?

The ever-precarious balance was again suddenly upset as I prepared to go home from college for Thanksgiving break that year. The news interrupted everything, and life came to a complete halt. President Kennedy had been assassinated in Dallas. How could such an unthinkable thing happen? What had we become? How could we ever recover? I had so many questions that were beyond just the loss of one life, even one that had made such a difference in the lives of so many.

The rest of that fall was numbing. I barely had enough interest or energy to finish my first semester of college. It felt like the hope that had been building had evaporated in one brief instant. There didn't seem to be much to look forward to. This loss represented the worst of what we had allowed our society to tolerate.

That New Year's Eve, Malcolm X, after adding even more controversy to his civil rights leadership, was finally able to clarify what he meant when he said after the assassination, "The chickens have come home to roost." There had been many interpretations of his words, but when the press was able to ask him directly, he explained that what he meant was that it was the result of a climate of hate, that violence had become a way of life in America.

In 1964 it was extremely difficult to garner any semblance of hope, even when President Johnson announced that his War on Poverty would strike at the causes, not just the consequences, and would provide numerous opportunities for underprivileged Americans to develop skills and continue their education, and for others to volunteer in this effort.

I was skeptical when the Civil Rights Act became legislation, outlawing discrimination of any kind. Can a law change behaviors, attitudes, and values that have persisted for so many generations? Something more—something different—was needed to change people's hearts. That summer, circumstances took a dramatic turn for the worse. What was to be the Freedom Summer to increase voter registration started off with three more civil rights workers getting killed in Mississippi.

Within weeks, the Tonkin Gulf Resolution, anything *but* a resolution, gave President Johnson the authority to wage war against North Vietnam without any checks or balances. This was the beginning to legitimizing a long and extremely costly war upon a people that we did not understand for reasons most Americans did not understand either.

One bright spot before this year came to an end was Martin Luther King Jr.'s being awarded the Nobel Peace Prize.

But 1965 began with another needless assassination. During his pilgrimage to Mecca, Malcolm X met whites for the first time who were not racist, who saw themselves as part of the human family. Transformed, having seen firsthand how people of different colors and backgrounds not only got along but experienced the truth of unity, he returned to the United States with a new perspective, determined to spread a new message: that our problem is "not an American problem, it's a human problem; not a Negro problem, it's a problem of humanity; not a problem of civil rights, but of human rights." But he was not given the chance to carry it any further. Who *would* champion this message, I wondered.

This was my sophomore year in college, and I made the decision to major in philosophy. There was a new world beginning to open up before me, and I wanted to pursue studies that most intrigued me, that would offer me some answers, or at least help me formulate the right questions. My new major gave me glimpses into classic and modern philosophy and opened up my interests in classic mythology and comparative religion as well.

At the same time, civil rights marches from Selma to Montgomery continued, and antiwar protests escalated in Washington and other places, as Operation Rolling Thunder began a program of bombing in North Vietnam that led to the massive killing of civilians, while U.S. ground forces in Vietnam went on the offensive for the first time.

That summer, more race riots ensued. In Watts, rage and pillaging tore Los Angeles—and the country—apart for nearly a week. What sense did any of this fear, hatred, and violence make? I couldn't help but ponder these perplexing times.

In 1966, when the Equal Employment Opportunity Commission failed to enforce the provision of the Civil Rights Act prohibiting discrimination in employment based on gender, twenty-eight women at the annual Conference of the Commission on the Status of Women founded the National Organization for Women "to bring women into the mainstream of American society now . . . in fully equal partnership with men," effectively seeking to fulfill a 120-year-old vision.

The summer saw additional race riots in Atlanta and Cleveland, and by the end of that year, Martin Luther King Jr. made his opposition to the war public, while newspapers reported that women were the next great issue for civil rights and that the days of male supremacy were numbered.

In 1967, a month before my college graduation, hundreds of thousands of protesters, including Martin Luther King Jr., demonstrated at the United Nations in New York. I knew that *I* needed a change at this time, too, not only from my campus, but also from the East Coast to the West Coast. I applied, got accepted, and was eager to begin my graduate work at the University of Washington.

Right after graduation, I drove out to Seattle and started my studies in a field I thought I wanted to pursue, library science. But after a month of beginning to learn how to catalog books, I realized that I really wanted to try my hand at writing them instead. I dropped out at the end of June and took the long route home.

I headed south, through Oregon and to California. I was going to San Francisco, having heard Scott McKenzie's song many times. Drawn first to the corners of Haight and Asbury, I joined in the flow of the throngs of young people. Some were handing out a "Safe Conduct Pass" for making it through the rumored "love-in" there. The pass informed recipients that "this is the first day of the rest of your life."

I went on to explore the rest of the neighborhood around the Panhandle of the Golden Gate Park, gain-ing a real taste of what was going on at the heart of a new culture during the summer of love.

With a renewed sense of expectation, I headed back to New York. But I soon heard all about the race riots in Detroit, Newark, and more than a hundred other cities that summer.

Despite the many distractions, I managed to think a bit about what I was going to do next and serendipitously came upon an announcement of a new graduate program in American folk culture. I knew immediately I wanted to pursue this, and I started the program right away in September.

My new studies drew me right in to what they had to offer, but trying to stay focused became difficult as news of the Tet Offensive, launched by the Vietcong at Nha Trang in January of 1968, spread.

Walter Cronkite, reporting on his trip to Vietnam in the aftermath of the Tet Offensive, called for negotiations to end the war. This message coming from a trusted news anchor helped even more to move public support further away from the war in Vietnam.

By early April it felt like hope had once again been lost, surrendered to the scourge of senseless violence. The illustrious life of the foremost spokesperson of non-violence for this generation, Martin Luther King Jr., came to a devastating end. The image of his friends and associates on the balcony of the motel pointing to where the shots came from is still fresh in my mind.

Senator Robert Kennedy, just before he was to give a speech during his campaign for the presidency, urged the crowd, and America, in his impromptu eulogy "to tame the savageness of man and make gentle the life of this world."

Two months later, the assassination of Senator Kennedy himself cut short his bid to unite a fractured nation. Once again, a shocking event changed the direction of the flow of things and caused a bookful of unanswerable questions in my mind. Fittingly, as his body was transported by train across America, along the tracks of the towns and cities, thousands of people spontaneously appeared, all standing in silent tribute.

With so much madness already that year, it was not surprising that the demonstrations against the war turned violent in Chicago and received more attention than the Democratic Convention itself going on there.

The year closed with Richard Nixon's being elected as the next president by a sliver of a margin of the popular vote on a platform of "law and order" and the promise that "the long dark night for America is about to end."

My flood of memories brought me back to 1969, which had started off with a series of violent campus uprisings spreading from one side of the country to the other. The April issue of *Rolling Stone*, with its cover on "American Revolution 1969" and the image of a bloodied protester with his head on the ground at the mercy of a billy club-wielding policeman, mirrored what we were living through.

I knew I would never forget that just two months before I had lost a childhood and high school friend, Wayne Meyer, to the war in Vietnam. Remembering the times that helped us grow—childhood birthday parties, Cub Scouts, adventures in the woods, overnights at the cottage on the Sound, Boy Scouts, our first adventure out of town on our three-speed bikes across the Sound on the ferry and into Connecticut and back, and more—I prayed for his soul, grateful for the memories but deeply saddened for his ultimate sacrifice.

≈≈≈

It was difficult, almost painful, to come back into the present after this seemingly endless torrent of ups and downs. I tried to quiet my mind for a moment, to rest from the ongoing rush of all that I had recalled, trying to be still with all that had happened. The war *was* on my mind all the time, but my heart tried to keep me where I was in each moment.

I remembered Pete Seeger's song with the holistic perspective from Ecclesiastes, "To everything there is a season, and a time to every purpose under Heaven . . . a time to love and a time to hate; a time for war and a time for peace." The only sentiment he added to these wise words echoed mine exactly: it's not too late.

My thoughts raced on. Things happened during the '60s that will mark me forever, a moment in time that has altered a lifetime. It had been a decade that changed a generation, for better or for worse. I knew there was a power to these songs of the '60s and that I must continue to resist whatever would hold me back from helping to bring about the progress so necessary to our well-being. I knew I must contribute in some way to whatever would promote justice, not just for one but for everyone.

The world was no longer so big and distant. I was growing ever-more conscious of being connected to everything else. One of the things I learned from the moonwalk, and my reflection on the '60s, was simply that the whole is greater than the sum of its parts. The decade had given me much cause for concern, and even despair, but the overall import of it as a whole is that much progress was made, even though at a huge cost, and much is still needed.

The moonwalk, capping this lurching yet luminous decade coming to a close, was surely a giant leap for humanity; it gave me much hope.

From this perspective, it is as if an old, decaying—perhaps dying—order was convulsing while a new world view was gradually being born.

I knew I was at the cusp of a great change of my own. But I wondered: What is in store for me? Is my direction known? Can hope truly continue? And I fell asleep that wondrous night quite content.

In the morning, after the campers began their activities, Richard and I had a chance to process what we were experiencing. Through our struggle as advocates for the campers, we had found an affinity of purpose. We each had a sense of what was in the other's thoughts before we spoke.

When he told me he had already decided to leave the camp, I was not surprised. What he had wanted to accomplish was no longer possible here. I was still unsure whether I would stay or not.

"Part of me feels disillusioned, too," I confided, "but another part of me is hopeful." This moment recalled for me the first time I had ever heard my "inner voice" and drew its message right out into the open. I knew I could share my most intimate conviction with Richard and that he would understand my deeper dilemma. "Since I was a child, I have wanted to know our Creator. I'm sure there is a purpose to life. I must find my role in it."

"Our dreams hold glimpses into the future," he whispered.

"Today, with the moonwalk, we have seen ourselves as never before," I continued. "We have been given a fresh glimpse of reality. Our world has changed right before our eyes. Yet in the next moment, we are right back where we were before. How can we balance these two realities? There is so much more to know."

"Our way of transcending even the subtlest of limits," he said, "is by following our dreams."

"But I feel torn," I told him. "I don't know whether to remain here, go with you, or embark on my own quest."

"Greatest is the dream that awakens those of others. Hold on to yours," he advised.

That exchange connected us like never before. We both knew that I would leave the camp too.

Feeling certain I'd be guided to the right destination, I slept well that evening. In the morning, I knew clearly what my next step should be. I would turn in my resignation and spend a few days with Richard at his parents' summer cottage on the island nearby. There we would reflect together on what had just happened and on what we could have done differently to enrich the campers' experience.

We took the short ferry ride across the bay and arrived at his cottage, which was situated in a beautiful spot by the water's edge. After a sail around the bay, we plunged into the business at hand: developing a deeper understanding of ourselves, where we had come from, and where we were going.

We decided to approach this task methodically. We would take turns guiding each other on a twenty-four hour inner exploration, free of distractions and other concerns.

We began with Richard as the explorer and me as the guide. I would accompany him wherever he went on this inner journey, supporting him, accepting and validating what he had to say, and encouraging him to continue. Our goal was to become better acquainted with our souls so we would know where we would be going next.

The first day, which we spent both inside the house and outside on the lawn overlooking the bay, was filled with hard work, some scares, many insights, and new understandings. I both followed and led him where he needed most to go, and it felt more like an eternity than a day.

On the second day, Richard guided me to the depths and heights, the shadows and lights, of my being. Though we didn't see everything the same way, we deeply respected each other's truths.

The first mystery I explored was the meaning of my life. To know myself, I realized I would have to know my parents better. I would have to take a long look at how they had influenced me.

Most important was their love. Did I feel it? Did I ever doubt it? As I reflected on this, I remembered that though they didn't openly say it, they did express their love often and in many ways: the trips taken just for me, their only child, the support given me even when I didn't know I needed it, and the constant little things they did for me. Their love was ever-present and always felt but unspoken.

I also wanted to know the meaning of my own silence. There were times, long after my stuttering had diminished, that I wanted to speak but held back. Nothing in our family was secret, yet little was openly affirmed. My mom spoke freely, while my dad would say he liked to hear other people's opinions first and weigh them all. Through the years, they learned to appreciate each other just as they were.

I wondered what was preventing me from speaking my truth. Sometimes I had little chance to speak and other times my mom drew the words right out of me. My dad once said something that really stuck: "If you can't say something good about a person, don't say anything at all."

My lesson in this exercise of self-reflection was that I needed to make an extra effort to speak my own mind, to act confidently, and to be more daring. Most important, I saw that I would have to work hard to break out of my pattern of silent retreat; I needed to assert myself to create my own destiny.

I was aware of my parents' gifts to me, some that had been handed down across generations; so it was that I had become quietly persistent. Yet I knew that to become my true self I had to free myself, at least temporarily, from their mold.

Perhaps, like my dad, I had been content to listen to others. Yet, I had to learn how to identify the situations that can expand my inner self, possibly empower me and maybe even others, and learn how to find the courage to act on my instinct in such situations. This would be finding a middle ground between my parents' attributes.

I became poignantly aware that there would always be something within me that I would not be able to fully express as long as I was still in the process of becoming whole. There was a part of me yearning to be heard, longing to give birth to some new part of me. Whatever was preventing me from expressing more of myself was also getting in the way of realizing my potential.

If I surrendered to my silence, I might be able to speak. Similarly, if I surrendered my individual will to the universal will, I might feel a benevolent power aiding me in making the choices I faced, in connecting more deeply to others, and in adopting and holding the right attitudes in each situation. I was determined to place my trust in this larger will.

The insights gained and lessons learned made these two days the most intense and fruitful of my life. In giving our secrets and dreams over to each other, Richard and I shared more of what we really cared about than we even knew was there, and we discovered more about ourselves than we had ever imagined possible. We listened to each disclosure with compassion—being there, without judging, as a friend to each other's soul—respecting and trusting fully, giving and receiving equally, and in the process establishing a firm bond with each other.

By the second night I was refreshed and keenly aware that something more was awaiting me. I knew I had to follow my own path, wherever it might lead me. I also knew that I was embarking on a new beginning.

Early the next morning, I left Richard at the cottage on the island, took the ferry, and for a brief interlude wandered along the shoreline at Montauk with the wind at my back.

As though a weight had lifted from my shoulders, I felt hopeful again, eager to taste and touch my future. From observing my life close-up, I knew I could accept whatever might happen and be content with it.

The sea spray sparkled, gemlike, animating the world around me. Gulls with spread wings plunged into the bountiful waters and emerged with bits of nourishment. Rocks—some huddled together, some off on their own— stood firm against the onrushing tide. The waves washed ashore, singing of an eternal journey.

The sand dunes rising overhead sighted ships and birds, all the while catching the words of beachcombers. Steadfast, they watched the unveiling of the ever-changing sea beauty; theirs was a vision of universal order.

Again my inner voice spoke:

Let the day go by with no thought of time. What clock can confine eternity?

Does the flower growing in the sun check a timepiece every hour?

Time is the matron of evolution; its womb is the moment. Only the living moment reveals the wonder of eternity.

Come, let us go forth together, catching each moment as if it were a lifetime. There never was a moment more real than this one.

The morning sun was high above the sea as I wandered on, deep in thought. Soon I saw a circle of children playing in the sand dunes, lost in the joy of summer. At first I felt separate, alienated from them. What did I have in common with them? How could they be so absorbed in life's simplest pleasures?

Then I remembered that as a child I was not who I am today. I, like these children, had secret places that gave me joy, favorite spots in the woods, or along streams, that allowed me to feel at home. I, too, once had a sense of wonder and a carefree curiosity that pulled me to explore my surroundings.

As an only child, I was accustomed to being by myself and managed to find plenty to do. I much preferred, however, to be with others.

Drawn to this circle of children, I could see in them something authentic and oddly familiar—an aliveness and wakefulness I had to struggle to maintain. They had not yet lost their innocence. Their joy is the real thing, pure and unsullied. Perhaps I have left childish things behind too soon. I need to let my joy out and rediscover that eager, excited child within me.

So I joined them in a romp across the sandy beach; its softness awakened my toes, and I felt each grain as part of my boundless home. With the waves playing a soothing rhythm upon the shore, everything around me contributed to a natural harmony.

I gazed once more at the children drawing pleasure in the moment. And again my inner voice spoke:

Children, in their purity, are the ones with the open eyes; they see the mysteries clearly. A child's desire is the wind's desire, a mirror of the earth's movement.

Though the leaves are bound by the seasons, they flutter with joy in the summer breeze. Though the trees sleep in winter, they stand with inner certainty of their spring awakening.

Though the nightingale is blanketed by the skies, it soars in its own heaven. Within the ocean, the fish swim freely. What shackles have we, but those we strap onto ourselves?

Our greatest freedom lies in recognizing our connection with all of creation.

ASSISTANCE

Leaving my new young friends behind, I was eager to find my own way. Everywhere I went, it seemed that each twig, each leaf, was open to the warm call of life, eager to fulfill its promise, as was I in the summer of my soul.

One morning a local newspaper headline caught my eye: "Hudson River Sloop Arrives at Port Jeff Today."

I immediately remembered the year before when I had first met Pete Seeger, a friend of Harry Siemsen, the Catskill Mountain folksinger I had interviewed. Pete had given me some background information about Harry, and he also told me that he was raising money to build a replica of an old cargo sloop that had plied the river a century ago.

He and lots of other volunteers would sail her from port to port, teaching people to love their river again. The sloop was called the *Clearwater,* and it was run by the Hudson River Sloop Restoration, which Pete said was probably the first organization to have a bard as chairman of its board.

Recently launched in Maine, the *Clearwater* was on its way to New York City. This was my opportunity to see

Pete again and maybe sail on the sloop. But would he remember me? Would there be room for me? What would I do on board?

While my mind pondered these uncertainties, my heart knew where it wanted to be. So I headed for Port Jeff. Letting my courageous self take over, I found the sloop at the dock and spoke to Pete.

"Do you remember last year, when we talked about your project and you said I might be able to help? I really would like to. Maybe I could gather stories from people who can tell us what the river was like in the days of the sloops."

"I think you've got something there," the troubadour replied. "The history of the river should be told, too. We could use your help on that. Can you meet us in New York this weekend and sail with us so we can work out the plans?"

"I'd love to!"

I could hardly believe my ears. For three years Pete and his singing friends had given "sloop concerts" up and down the Hudson, raising money to build the *Clearwater* and save the river. His dream had come true, and now *I* was to have a part in it.

The next day, hundreds of people lined New York's South Street Seaport pier in a spectacular expression of support. Under a skyline draped in gray, a fleet of tugs, sailboats, and other launches surrounded the broad-beamed, green-hulled sloop. A single mast held its billowing white canvas aloft, and young seafarers stood proudly upon its deck.

The sloop glided into its berth as the crowd remained expectantly silent. Within moments Pete Seeger—the banjo-playing, mind-stretching, shelter-giving humanitarian—

bearded and wearing a sailor's cap, stepped up on the stage and surged forward in the breeze to share his vision.

"Who's going to clean up this river of ours? No polluter, no politician, is going to lift a finger unless we insist on it. So we have to make ourselves heard. We're all in this environmental thing together. Not even a millionaire can escape it. We've got to take action right now. We may have to start small, but each of us can do something. First, we can all do some reading. Get copies of the books we have here on the ship. Find out the facts about the environmental crisis. Then talk it up."

"The idea is simple," he continued. "We want people to come down to the river again. But the most important thing is to get together. Because we just won't make it unless we can talk to one another and agree on what we have to do. All of us. Young and old, black and white, rich and poor, longhair and crew cut. We hope people will say, 'Gee, this river is a mess. Ought to do something about it.' You see, everything in the world is tied together. You clean up a river, and soon you have to work on cleaning up society. Let's all get together and make this thing work. We can do it. Don't let anyone tell you we can't. But we have to want to do it!"

As he broke into song, "Sailing down my dirty stream," everyone could tell that he still loved the river and that he held high his dream that someday the Hudson would once again run clear.

When the music stopped, the people cheered, echoing his enthusiasm. Then the haze that had blurred the skyline slipped silently away.

I knew this was where I belonged. It was evident not only in what he had written around the edge of his banjo skin—"This machine surrounds hate and forces it to surrender"—but in how he embodied love in all that he did.

Later that afternoon I joined the other seafarers for the sloop's maiden voyage up the Hudson River. I was the newest crew member and the only nonsinging one. The others—"Ramblin'" Jack Elliott, Don McLean, Gordon Bok, Brother Fred Kirkpatrick, Jimmy Collier, Len Chandler, Lou Killen, Andy Wallace, Jon Eberhart, and Captain Alan Aunapu—had all performed on stage with Pete.

We sailed around the tip of Manhattan, passing the Statue of Liberty and entering the mouth of the river in a boat the people of the Hudson Valley hadn't seen in nearly a hundred years. I lay back, taking everything in.

That first day, skyscrapers and factories loomed overpoweringly from the shoreline. Clouds of smog hung over our heads. Conveyor-belt highways were teeming with cars driven by people who were themselves driven by the demands of time and place.

Our sloop meandered along at a pace set by winds and tides. It took most of the day to reach the George Washington Bridge at the north end of the bustling island. I thought of the travelers who had made this same voyage to Albany in the days when sloops carried real cargo as well as passengers. They must have seen lush grass and wildflowers growing along the shore and taken in the sweet smells coming from them.

That night, at anchor in a quiet cove after a delicious dinner from the *Clearwater* galley, most of us followed Allan, Jack, Lou, and Jimmy into the small hold below the foredeck.

There they sat around picking and singing whatever tunes came into their heads. Allan sang some Caribbean songs he had learned while sailing there; Jack let loose with some Woody Guthrie songs he had picked up while traveling with him. For hours we listened to songs, old and new, never wanting the music to stop. And I found that singing is not only a way of earning a living but, more importantly, a way of life.

The next day, the rock wall of the Palisades, topped with hemlocks, oaks, and tulip trees, towered over our little sloop like a natural fortress as we plied our course, drifting lazily along in an eternal flow.

But I began to wonder how I would fit into the routine of shipboard life. I felt out of place among seasoned seafarers, a stranger upon unfamiliar waters. They all knew their tasks, their roles. What about mine?

I asked Allan, our captain, who was as much a virtuoso on the ship's halyards as on his guitar strings, "How can I play an equal part in this community?"

Peering over the side of the ship with his golden locks flowing in the wind, he replied, "Listen to the music of the surrounding waters. The fish silently reveal a secret. They swim as one, sensing the spirit that binds them with their surroundings. With trust and a common will, they carry on as an endless wave in the sea of creation."

At that moment, in the Tappan Zee, the river valley came alive with the call of adventure.

Our every move was determined by a wind charged with power. We took a tack to starboard, and with a mighty slap, back came the mainsail, flapping loosely across the deck. A gust filled the canvas, and as we picked up our course on the port, the lines were pulled taut. Listing in a brisk gale, we headed for a cove, seeking safety as the ship's rail dipped below the sea spray.

At the foot of stern mountains, unseen streams roared down into the river. Amid the sea's ever-breathing energy I, the novice, began to feel more comfortable. I pitched in, hauling a line, and found my place within the seagoing community.

After the squall passed, I climbed out onto the bowsprit and rested in its hammock-like netting. There I regained a perspective on the sea's inner order.

Ahead lay Nyack, our first port of call, where we docked for a sloop festival. By sunset a few visitors were still aboard the sloop. Some were talking with crew members on deck while others were singing by the tiller as Allan played his guitar.

Sitting on the quarterdeck was a young lady in a wide-brim hat, gazing out over the river. She beckoned me with her soft, silent presence. But without knowing just what I would say, I walked over and greeted her, "Hi. Are you from around here?"

She looked up and smiled. We spoke for a few minutes. I learned her name was Judy and that she was home from college for the summer. We decided to leave the sloop for a walk in the park.

We soon came to a playground and jumped on the swings. After a while, we tried the seesaw, learning little bits about each other with every up-and-down movement of the plank. We walked up a hill, rolled down it, and lay in the warm grass, talking some more.

Later, as we headed back to the sloop, I said, "Hey, you know, this has been a real special night."

"Yeah, it has."

"I sail again tomorrow. We'll be in Albany by next weekend."

"That's the day of the festival," she said excitedly.

"That's right. We'll be doing another sloop festival there, too."

"No, I mean Woodstock!"

"Oh, that one. Are you going?"

"Yeah."

"Well, maybe we could meet there."

"They're expecting thousands of people," she exclaimed. "How would we ever find each other?"

"Easy. We'll meet in front of the stage at noon on Sunday."

"Well, I guess we could try it."

"Great," I said. "Don't forget."

"I won't. Well, I've got to find my little sister and get her home."

"It's been really nice. See you Sunday."

"Yeah. See you at Woodstock."

THRESHOLD

The sloop set sail early Monday morning, tacking through the storied hollow. I sat bare-chested, high upon the crosstree, bobbing to and fro.

The ship revealed to me a secret of the whole unto itself, caught in a purposeful yet unpredictable flow. Moving upon the waters in stately procession, all parts work together as a unit. For each rope that is pulled in, one is loosened.

The sea gives up secrets, too. Forever breathing droplets fall through my fingers, yet hold up the ship that glides upon its surface. The sea sleeps not, yet is endowed with life's eternal energy. I realized it is the magic of this perpetual motion that has lured me away from the land.

Sailing through the highlands, we gazed at the beauty of the river valley at its finest. Gently rolling mountains crowned with forests afforded a delightful contrast between the blue of the river and the sky.

Once in Albany, with the sloop safely moored, and after another local celebration, Allan, an old sailing buddy of

David Crosby, two other crew members, and I left late Saturday night for Woodstock to see for ourselves if this touted event was really about peace and music.

We arrived at Max Yasgur's farm, amidst the rolling fields, just before dawn, during a quiet moment between sets from the night before. The rumored closed highways were all clear, and we found very little movement at all but were quickly told by those we passed that it was now a free concert.

Everyone was settled in, spread out on the hill around the massive stage area, either sleeping or resting, right where they had been listening to the music all day and night. Those we found awake welcomed us with friendly faces.

Soon, upon the imposing stage, with towers of scaffolding holding aloft many speakers, we heard "Good morning people. It's a new dawn." And as Jefferson Airplane sang "The Other Side of This Life," I wondered, too, where am I going next, and who am I going to be?

It did seem as if this were the kind of setting where secrets would be shared and where both sides of life might become better known. I managed to find an open spot and sat down to enjoy the music.

A little later I eased my way toward the seemingly mile-long stage, careful not to step on anyone in the pathless mass, hoping to find my new friend Judy where we had planned to meet. Starting at one side, pressing up against the ten-foot high wood-slat fence guarding the stage, I inched along toward the middle, barely able to make it through the throngs of people pushing in. After what seemed like hours, I had made my way nearly to the other side, and there I spotted her coming toward me.

"You made it!" she cried.

"Yeah, this is absolutely incredible!" I replied.

"I know. I've never seen anything like it before."

As we turned and walked off to the side, Joe Cocker, with his bright tie-dyed shirt and spastic gyrations, sang what we all knew from our own experience of being there—we'll get by with a little help from our friends.

Before we had gotten too far, a torrent of rains came. We headed for her friend's tent to wait out the storm but never got there. From the stage came the announcement, "We're all in the same puddle, and we can work it out."

Stuck in the crowds amid the rain and mud, we found the people especially friendly. Each was looking out for the other and freely sharing what they had. There really was a sense of "we're all here together, let's make the best of it." It was exactly what a community should be like.

"It's really great being here," Judy announced to me. "This feels different, like the beginning of a whole new way of seeing things. This is going to change everything."

We enjoyed the people and the music for the rest of the day and evening. Our time together at Woodstock felt like weeks yet passed too quickly.

In the morning, I said, "This has been a lot of fun. It would be nice to see you again."

"Yeah, it has. I've enjoyed being with you. Let's keep in touch. I've got a little time before I have to get back to college."

We exchanged phone numbers and agreed to see if there might be a way we could meet before the summer was over.

As we walked toward the cars, I thought that these three days of peace and music were not in the least a diversion or even an escape from the ever-present pain of Vietnam and all the other senseless killings in our own land, but a reminder that time is always moving forward and that we all have to be continually seeking our own deeper presence, our own future, and our own meaning.

Reluctantly ready to leave this experience behind us, we could hear a quiet, but screeching, guitar piece that resembled "The Star Spangled Banner" coming from Jimi Hendrix.

My companions and I drove back to the sloop.

As we sailed back down river through waters pierced by the powerful prow, I gazed at the leaves along the shore sparkling in a backlit brightness and peered up at the puffs of clouds passing overhead. Old seamen, sitting on the pier and eager to relive the days of yore, gazed pensively as we glided by.

And the days on the river passed by, too. One day, approaching the Rip van Winkle Bridge, I took a turn at the tiller. I held it gingerly, not sure of the play in its motion. Soon I found that while holding this toothpick of a timber that guides the broad hull ahead and lofty mast above, I got a charge of energy and was able to keep the lumbering vessel true to her course.

Slipping under the bridge, I thought of old Rip and recognized that I, too, had broken out of a long slumber. It was as if I had just sailed into the realm of being, where I now became conscious of sensations and truths I had not known before. It was like entering another realm of existence, where awareness was heightened and primary, where the everyday things of this world mattered less, and the mysteries and wonders of life—its spiritual significance— mattered most.

This was a new and refreshing feeling; I sensed a clearer recognition of the vision that guided me and felt a stronger attraction to that force animating me. In fact, something had come alive within me, giving me greater access to the unknown in myself and to the mysteries of reality.

It felt like the beginning of the process of the unfolding of the seed in my soul. And just as with the dim light of the early dawn where the sun's path is sure to ascend upward, I felt confident that this process would continue from this day on.

In this summer of my awakening, I was getting in touch with my life and, after what seemed like a twenty-year sleep, I was feeling fully present. I saw how the moonwalk affirmed my sense that we are all one people on this planet. Then Pete Seeger reappeared in my life at just the right moment. His unwavering commitment to the most vital issues of our times—social justice, equality, peace, and environmental awareness—were a beacon of light to all and an inspiration to my soul. His concern and caring ways showed me that I mattered, that I fit into the picture, too. His support, encouragement, and guidance gave me much-needed confidence. I felt deeply grateful to have come into his presence.

And beyond this, I was finally feeling as if I could leave behind the effects of my stuttering. I had begun to emerge out of silence and to find and follow my own voice, but I knew that my journey to self-expression was just beginning.

Still holding the tiller and keeping the sloop on its path, my inner voice, with which I was becoming more familiar, silently uttered this prayer: *Gracious, ever-surging sea, gather together for me a few of your wisdom pearls, and spray them upon my soul. I shall gladly accept them as seeds of everlasting understanding, tokens from your ocean of infinite meaning.*

As night fell, we dropped anchor in the serenity of a moonlit tide. The creaking in the rigging, the water gently lapping the hull, a fully brightened moon, and passing clouds occasionally dimming its light, all added to the awe of a perfectly ordered evening.

Though the direction of my life was becoming gradually clearer, I knew that I would still have to face long-dormant parts of myself. With that thought and a cool wind coming on, I could do no better than sleep, nestled peacefully in the furled sail, rising and falling with the breathing tide.

Fall

A brisk wind blew upon the Hudson, the tide ran cooler, the leaves began to shiver, the days grew shorter, and billowy clouds filled the sky. With a stream of watery experiences behind me and the path ahead unknown, I was caught in contemplative abeyance.

Where I was going became secondary to where I had come from. As earth and sky went their separate ways, it was time for me to leave the sea so I could feel the beating of my heart and find the peace of my own silence. With no expectations other than to know myself better, I began to look for a quiet place nearby where I could reflect further on my path.

Retreat

It didn't take long to find my desired sojourn. Pete told me about an empty cabin just down the mountainside from his home. He gave me the name of the owner, I called, and, sure enough, it was available. I went right over to look at it.

The small two-room cabin seemed a perfect home base for carrying out the interviews I had arranged with the people in the river towns we had sailed to. It offered a convenient mid-valley location and was set back off the road, only a short walk through the woods to the Hudson River.

I moved in that day. I chopped and stacked logs for the fireplace and quickly got the lay of the land, which included a stream that ambled down the hillside to the river. Then I began to settle in.

I had cold running water but no toilet. Behind the cabin was a privy. The kitchen and living room formed one room with a huge rough-stone fireplace; the bedroom was the only other room.

Before I knew it, I was struck by an acute sense of aloneness. Not being close to anyone special became very real once more. I was forced to face this sensation head-on. That night I had a restless sleep.

In the morning, thoughts of being alone overtook me again. Stepping out into the woods, I recalled the many pleasant hours I had played alone as a child. Yet my dream of union with another was still strong. Shedding their leaves around me, the trees offered a response I was not ready for: I have been left alone to discover myself!

I knew I could not let this insight go unattended. I could not let my self slip away again. My job in this world of silence was to find signs of, and connect further with, my teachers and mentors, those around me and those within me.

I realized fully that this time alone was indeed a gift, a time to go deeper into what I already knew, and to un-cover what was waiting for me, all around me. I knew I had to settle in to my abode by reconnecting with those who had already inspired me.

I unpacked my carton of well-worn books that made up my essential library and put them on the shelf. The first book I took off the shelf was the poet of Paumanok, Walt Whitman, who had already taught me that his inner world connected him to everyone:

I celebrate myself,
And what I assume you shall assume,
For every atom belonging to me as good belongs to you.

He was full of apparent contradictions: "Clear and sweet is my Soul, and clear and sweet is all that is not my Soul. . . ."

Yet he was also a master of juxtaposing the clash of oppos-ing forces to illustrate something greater than the parts. He spoke not of a temporal, ever-changing realm but of one that does not waver, even with the blowing winds of time. He, with questing eyes, recognized permanency beyond change.

I believe in you, my Soul—the other I am must not abase itself to you,
And you must not be abased to the other.

Whitman, the singer of the yet unsung, was the poet whom he thought Emerson had looked for, the reconciler of opposites. He taught me of the wholeness of the creation behind its parts, of the continuity across and between the realms of creation, and gave me the courage to always look past the ambiguity of the moment.

All goes onward and outward—nothing collapses;
And to die is different from what any one supposed, and luckier.
. . . .

I pass death with the dying, and birth with the new-wash'd babe and am not contain'd between my hat and boots.
. . . .

I am the mate and companion of people, all just as immortal and fathomless as myself.
. . . .

And I call to mankind, Be not curious about God,
For I who am curious about each am not curious about God;
(No array of terms can say how much I am at peace about God, and about death.)
. . . .

I hear and behold God in every object, yet I understand
God not in the least. . . .

. . . .

Do you see, O my brothers and sisters?
It is not chaos or death—it is form and union and plan—
it is eternal life—it is Happiness.

Walt Whitman showed me that there was much more
to life than what we encounter on this earth. And his thinking seemed to establish a direct link back to that of William Blake, whose *Poetry and Prose* I took off my shelf:

To see a World in a Grain of Sand
And a Heaven in a Wild Flower,
Hold infinity in the palm of your hand
And Eternity in an hour.

Next I reached for *Memories, Dreams, Reflections.* Perhaps Carl Jung had come to similar insights as he looked
back over and explored mainly the "inner experiences" of
his long and productive life.

Like every other being, I am a splinter of the infinite
deity. . . .
I am astonished, disappointed, pleased with myself. I
am distressed, depressed, rapturous. I am all these at once.
. . . I know only that . . . I exist on the foundation of
something I do not know. In spite of all uncertainties, I
feel a solidity underlying all existence and a continuity in
my mode of being. The world into which we are born is
brutal and cruel, and at the same time of divine beauty.

For Jung, too, there were seeming contradictions and opposing forces, but all led to a greater whole. Jung quoted Lao-tzu to sum up how he felt in the late evening of his life. "All are clear, I alone am clouded." And I could feel somewhat comforted in the late morning of my own life.

Early the next day, with a mixture of anticipation and trepidation, I ventured further into the woods. Reaching to the ground, I picked up a fallen leaf and blew it into the air. As it flew, I followed. Over stones and thorns I bounded, all the way down to the riverfront, where the leaf landed at my feet. The scenery before me was beautiful and peaceful, except for an occasional train.

Gazing into the clear water, I saw my own face mirrored, with an expression somewhere between joy and sorrow. My heart knew I must remain alone for as long as this took; my mind was prepared for deep reflection.

Questions resurfaced, ongoing quandaries I had not allowed myself to fully explore before, and for which I had no answers: Why am I so alone? Where am I going? What should I be doing? How will I find meaning in my life?

These questions brought me to a full stop. With a sobering awareness, I saw fully that the life I had been living was not all mine, not entirely of my choosing. Many of my decisions felt like those that others might have made for me. And I realized then that with many choices, I must be sure to make my actions my own.

What am *I* capable of? How can I fulfill *my* potential? Pondering these dilemmas, I vowed that I must seek the answers for myself, no matter how long it might take.

Another question arose: What have been the circumstances of my greatest victory, my most profound wonder, my deepest gratitude? Such experiences occurred, I remembered, when I was most open to what was happening around me, when I was fully present to take in the significance of even the most seemingly inconsequential event. That has been when I have recognized the wonder and the truth inherent in the moment and have been most grateful for it.

And yet another question posed itself: What is calling me? This one demanded further reflection. After many quiet moments, I realized that I must more fully seek to explore the mysteries of my life and the universe around me. This would surely lead me to my own inner truth and clarify my own purpose. Maybe then this could serve me in helping others to live into their truth. If I could become a guide to others in their search for truth, this was a task I knew would bring me great joy. I resolved then and there to make this the focus of my every thought.

With this as my goal, with this providing the meaning in my life, what room could be left for fear? Being alone could be my lot at any time, but I would welcome it rather than attempt to fight it or control it. Living fully in the moment, each moment would show me who I really am, what I am capable of, and where my dreams can take me.

Looking up at the azure sky, I felt the presence of something that linked me to the entire world. Turning my gaze back to the water, I saw my reflection once again. This time with an expression closer to assurance, I knew that I could call upon my own muse for the inspiration I would need.

Indeed, with all the life forms about me also alone yet firm and assured of their place, I, too, could be content just knowing that I was in touch with the greatest teacher, nature, in all her exquisite forms.

That evening, in the shelter of my retreat, I settled in to reread Thoreau, who had inspired me to seek the solace of the surrounding woods. If there ever was anyone who knew how to live in the present moment wherever he was, it was the tenant of Walden Pond.

Live each season as it passes; breathe the air, drink the drink, taste the fruit, and resign yourself to the influence of each. . . .

I went to the woods because I wished to live deliberately, to front only the essential facts of life, and see if I could not learn what it had to teach, and not, when I came to die, discover that I had not lived. . . .

In proportion as he simplifies his life, the laws of the universe will appear less complex, and solitude will not be solitude, nor poverty poverty, nor weakness weakness.

Thoreau was a seeker from childhood, when he first gazed into the sky at night, looking beyond the stars, wanting to see God behind them. Every day he made some new acquaintance with Nature, as Emerson had noted in his eulogy to his neighbor.

And Emerson's own *Self-Reliance,* a longtime staple in my collection of wisdom works, spoke to my inner essence.

Accept the place the Divine Providence has found for you. . . . He who would gather immortal palms must not be hindered by the name of goodness, but must explore if it be goodness. . . . Good and bad are but names very readily transferable to that or this. . . . A man is to carry himself in the presence of all opposition as if everything were titular and ephemeral. . . . When a man lives with God, his voice shall be as sweet as the murmur of the brook and the rustle of the corn.

There is also, in Emerson, a purpose in the clash of opposites and a strong sense of an underlying natural order to everything in which we, whether we realize it or not, fit right in and are an integral part.

Before I called it a night, I wanted to go further back in time to see if I could find any other threads in this fascinating weaving of holistic thinking. I pulled off my shelf the *I Ching,* the ancient Chinese book of changes, with its linear images of all that happens in heaven and on earth, depicting the organic processes unfolding in nature, a book of seasoned wisdom in which both Confucianism and Taoism find their roots.

The many possible combinations of lines, broken and unbroken, represent the state of continual change taking place in the physical world and the tendencies or characteristics found in such movement—a series of possible situations, each with clear counsel for appropriate action to be taken.

I realized that by actively participating in this combination of process and intervention in my own life, by recognizing the organic nature of my own life unfolding in its own way as one ongoing process, with change above the surface and steadiness beneath the surface, that I could share in the creation of my own destiny.

As Confucius had said, standing by a river, "Everything flows on and on like this river, without pause, day and night." Richard Wilhelm's introduction to the *I Ching* gave me an even deeper understanding of the idea of change, revealing what I would consider one of life's greatest gifts, that beyond all the change of this world lies a stillness, a oneness, that changes not. Before change came into this world, there was only the changeless. This primal beginning is represented by the circle, the original oneness, while the changes of this world are represented by the circle divided into the light and the dark, the yin and the yang. Duality came into the world, splitting the primal oneness into an above and a below, a right and a left, a front and back, a world of opposites.

Wilhelm said, "He who has perceived the meaning of change fixes his attention no longer on transitory individual things but on the immutable, eternal law at work in all change." This is the eternal law of the Tao, the principle of the one in the many, or the unity of opposites. Change is but the continuous transformation of the one form into its opposite, as night into day; such is the nature of the universal law that links us all to both the oneness of heaven and the dualities of earth.

Understanding the *I Ching* as nourishment for my soul, without further hesitation I opened the book randomly to hexagram 61, Chung Fu, or Inner Truth. I read the judgment. The image of the gentle wind above the joyous lake brings good fortune. It furthers one to cross the great stream.

Perseverance

Early the next morning, I awoke with an eagerness to again venture in through the wooded spires and wend my way to the mountainside stream. The night rain had transformed it into a spring of nourishment with an energy all its own. It roared down the hillside, announcing its strength to all creatures in the vicinity.

Drawn to its animating motion, I knelt down to meet the rushing stream, blocked a portion of it with my hand, and drank its crystal waters, an elixir to my thirsty soul. As I swallowed, I gazed around me, then toward the treetops, and newfound beauty spread before me. It was as if every molecule of existence burst alive.

With a sharper, clearer vision, I saw for the first time aspects of the world that had always been in front of me. I felt a renewed love for all of life and a wonder that, uniting me with the pulse of life, sang a song of sweetness to my awakened body.

When I am open to receiving even the simplest surprises, when I am closest to nature's heartbeat, I am able to come face-to-face with the wisdom of the universe. Nature, in her renewed splendor, continually answers even my un-asked questions.

Standing before her in contemplation, I find beauty, mystery, and eternal truth. This is the wonder that shall keep alive my deepest awe. And I felt for the first time that my life was mine and that this moment could last a lifetime.

Further into the woods, I came to a mighty waterfall pounding its way to a small pond below. Imbued with new courage, I waded into the pond and resolutely approached the majestic falls. I looked up in anticipation of making my ascent.

The chilly, plummeting drops began beating upon my face. As my vision blurred, I turned my thoughts inward. I saw the powerful falls as a myriad of singly falling drops, each one as important as the whole. Only in unity did they exert an influence beyond their individual limits.

A surge within propelled me onward, inch by inch, up the stone wall and into the tower of falling water. I began to pull my way over the protruding rocks until I reached the top.

Here I understood that only in its entirety does a goal appear overwhelming. Each conscious step we take toward where we want to be turns our volition into action and our intentional communion with nature into our deepest understanding. The unfolding of nature can clarify the mysteries of our own lives, as our inner workings are a reflection of the same universal law.

The waterfall made it clear to me; if a path to a goal appears too rough, we must attempt to go on anyway, as we will strengthen ourselves by overcoming the obstacles that seemed insurmountable from a distance, or we will discover new paths to either the initial goal or an equally rewarding one, or we may even find that there is something unknown impeding our progress, which then becomes a new goal to overcome.

Seeing eternity with my next step, I claimed the peace of the surrounding woods as mine. I found the creatures of nature happy with the way life is; we hear no complaints from them. The birds are constantly singing. The leaves are brightest just before their fall; they go gloriously. The bee gathers only honey, the sweet nectar of life. The brook, stumbling over many rocks, keeps on going. The tree, swaying in the wind, stands tall in its place.

Though my path would abound with valleys, I knew the peak of the distant mountain was part of me, too. In a land of hunger, I would feel nourished. In the silence of the morn, I would hear a song. In my soul I knew that, like the river flowing in its bed, I would be guided onward.

I waded out of the water, and in a moment of autumn ease, sat beside the swiftly flowing stream. As my mind stilled, I thought of my summer rendezvous with the young lady in the wide-brim hat.

I reflected on what this serendipitous encounter meant to me and realized its significance was of a promise of what might be, sometime in the future, if my good fortune were to continue.

We had gone our own ways, but I was grateful for what she had reawakened within me, not only the longing for an enduring love, but also the recognition that it is an abiding love of the infinite that would make such a love possible. This love is the promise of the soul.

And I reflected further that, only through relationships with others where individual differences emerge each moment, could I truly learn more about my soul. And only in a relationship with another, where circles of interactions expand ever outward, could my soul's promise be fulfilled. Such is the paradox of love. We ascend to the love of the sacred by being better able to recognize that which endures. All relationships go through seasons, but only the most mature experience the renewal of springtime. Love is the bridge between the physical and the spiritual worlds, between the temporal and the eternal.

For the first time, the obvious became clear. Being in love means being loving. Love is care and concern in action. To be loving requires a conscious effort to move beyond the hurdles that come our way while being in love.

The mystery of love is the great mystery of life. Love's challenge has shown me the value of a love that carries my soul to its loftiest perches. I vowed to seek a sacred love, one founded upon a shared vision, a union of spirits, and service to others. I vowed to continue to dream, to live into a love that knows no boundaries.

GRACE

My inner gleanings reminded me of the explorations of the soul I had begun with Richard at the summer cottage. There had been times since then when we had wanted to get together but didn't. So I drove out to see him on Cape Cod, where we quickly caught up on each other's adventures.

He, too, had been delving into dimensions he knew little about and had been finding pieces of his truth in many different places. He had studied with a psychic, lived on a commune, and worked with a clairvoyant. I was as fascinated by his awakenings as he was by mine.

After our visit, I decided to take a walk. Sauntering along the shore where earlier pilgrims had widened their horizons, I came to a spot where heaven and earth converged, where the creative and receptive merged.

In a momentary pause of equilibrium, I gazed into the afternoon sky. The sun was hiding behind a rainbow of myriad-hued clouds. But in an instant, the clouds opened before me, transforming into one pure white luminous light. An embrace of warmth engulfed my entire body. A ray of compassion reached in to fill my heart. I felt the imminence of divinely inspired renewal, as real as my own breath.

Reflecting further, I recognized this as the day that the "voice" had spoken to me of so long ago, when I would come to know God. In this awareness, I knew that I could know no greater purpose than returning my love to its source.

Yet I knew also, even though I *had* recognized this fateful day, that it was but a beginning to an endless lifelong quest to seek to understand the divine mysteries of creation. I also knew that I would continue to grow only as I am able to give back what I had been given.

I said good-bye to Richard again and began the long drive home. That night, I sat by the fire in quiet meditation.

Right away, my mind became very still, listening. Each thought that came and left reminded me that thoughts have lives of their own. Some had led me away from myself, while others spoke of qualities just waiting to emerge from within me. Some kept me within the space-time continuum marked by beginnings and endings, while others catapulted me into the timeless realm of eternity.

Clearly, it was up to me to determine the direction I would take, to turn toward the light meant to guide me. For this, I needed to identify the thoughts that were most deeply mine, most connected to the source of my being. I also needed to remain fully conscious each moment of my waking hours.

I hoped that there would be nothing to prevent me from feeling so in touch all the time. Perhaps in childhood I knew of this connectedness; now I needed to recapture it by attending to the present even more and honoring it without judgment, by seeing everything in its magnificence. I needed to slow down even more so I could see all that was before me and let it reveal its fullest and deepest meaning to me.

I realized that I had been thinking eternal thoughts, thoughts that could serve as beacons upon my path, and that I could think without thinking and have thoughts without thought, thus sustaining the inner quiet that leads to joy.

Then a beautiful tune, with notes of life giving to life, echoed softly. And the familiar voice of timelessness said:

There is but one song to sing, one song to be heard, one song that harmonizes all other notes now and for all time. That is the song of love. For the love of all life is the continuum along which we evolve.

Had I not been awake to this moment, such an understanding would have passed me by. But now I had a new burden, which caused me to reflect further. Could my deeds ever match my thoughts and words? In exchange for this understanding, what would I have to give up? What had I done to be deserving of this gift?

I knew that these questions would be answered in time. Meanwhile, I could but walk humbly, fully aware that profundity dwells in the mundane and that the best way to do something for myself would be to do something for others.

Stepping outside and meandering down the hill, I exulted in the feeling of peace within me, despite the changes taking place around me. Crisp, sorrel-painted leaves began to lose their hold and tumble slowly down, deliberately seeking their roots—a sure sign that the season of color had passed its crowning glory.

That night, with a cool wind coming, the woodpile next to my cabin was depleted noticeably, yet I had much to give thanks for. I listened for the music of the spheres to ring its clarion call and guide my soul.

The next day I drove my red VW Bug into the city for a reunion with Jack Elliott, who was playing at the *Gaslight Café*. Wearing his cowboy hat and spinning yarns of sailing, he sang with a style that made the cigarette smoke in the small basement club seem as if it were coming from a pile of freshly raked autumn leaves. His finger-picking was precise and punctuated, and his delivery detached yet determined.

Jack had brought along his wife, Martha; their baby, Aiyana; and Martha's friend, Wren. During one number, while walking around the tables singing, Jack spotted some old friends and urged them to follow him back to the stage. One of them was Len Chandler.

Also in the audience that night was another old friend, who yelled out from the back of the room, "You're getting worse every time I see you."

Jack returned the compliment from the stage, "That was Dave van Ronk. Every time I sing a song like 'Cocaine,' 'He Was a Friend of Mine,' or some other equally bad tune, I have to give him credit."

After the show, we reminisced about our adventures on the sloop. Jack had a few days off before his next gig on the

West Coast, and we decided to get in a couple of days of sailing on the *Clearwater.*

Early the next morning, Jack, Martha, Aiyana, Wren, and Bill, another of Jack's old sailing buddies, all piled into my VW Bug to find the sloop. But first Jack had called his pal Arlo Guthrie at his new farm in the Berkshires to see if he wanted to come sailing with us. Arlo said he was busy waiting for the gas man to come and invited us to come up to his place. We decided to do both: sail during the day and see Arlo later that night.

Off we drove along Canal Street and up West Side Highway. Soon the fanciful stories that made Jack a singer's singer started flowing. Bill remembered a talk-song that Jack did, a Ustinov thing on the Grand Prix, and asked him if he remembered it.

"Oh yeah," he replied. "You remember that thing? Man, that was in 1962. I was just back from Europe. Bob Dylan was living with me in that house where you brought the stuff in off your boat. Number One Sheridan Square. Did you ever get up there?"

"Sure, I remember that," Bill said.

A little while later, as I downshifted, Jack announced to all passengers: "The sound you have just heard is the normal sound of gearing down. Volkswagen Airlines wants you to be happy. Next time fly Volkswagen."

I thought of one of Jack's favorite pastimes and asked, "How did you get started climbing the rigging of ships?"

"I started doing that in 1949, when I was going to school at the University of Connecticut. I used to hitchhike up to the Mystic Marine Museum where the Concord and the Morgan are. It was a cold winter day and there were no people in the museum, so I didn't worry about being chased. They have signs up: Do Not Climb the Rigging. Disregarding these, I jumped into the whaler's fo'c'sle, changed into my Superman costume, and then up the ladder I flew. A quick glance over the shoulder, no one coming, I climbed up to the rigging. Mounting the lower shrouds, I climbed, hand over hand, foot over foot—hand on the shrouds, feet on the rattlings. I had been instructed by an old sailor man who said, 'When you climb aloft, sailor laddie, you always hold on to something vertical with your hand, some part of the fixed rigging. . . .'"

Jack, true to his name, rambled on for about twenty minutes solid, with an amazing discourse on all the technical aspects of the rigging of ships until he interrupted himself while crossing the Bear Mountain Bridge, "Look at the Hudson River at Bear Mountain," he said. "Have you ever seen this? It's one of the most beautiful rivers in America; Columbia, Snake, Colorado, Missouri."

We crossed more bridges and took every road that went along the river. Finally, as the sun was setting on a day that flew by, we found the *Clearwater* in New Hamburg.

After saying hello to everyone, we sat down to a delectable dinner from the sloop galley. Then we had a decision to make: were we going to sail or see Arlo? We looked at one another with indecision and decided to call Arlo once again to see if he could get away for a sail.

While Allan was talking to Arlo, Jack sang the old mainsail-raising song "Bound for South Australia" to get

Arlo in the mood. That didn't work. He still did not want to leave his farm.

After talking it over, we decided that Jack, Martha, Aiyana, and I would head to the Berkshires to see Arlo while Bill and Wren sailed the sloop back to New York.

On the way to Arlo's farm, Jack remarked, "This is the first time we've had a fun trip. All the others were for gigs."

Then he told us of one of his longtime wishes: "Some day I'm gonna build my own ship. David Crosby bought himself a fifty-two foot schooner off the money from 'Mr. Tambourine Man.' He first learned that song off a record by Bobby Dylan. Allan sailed with David Crosby on his schooner. Last time I met David—the only time I've ever spoken to him—he showed me a picture of the schooner he bought. He had a big brown paper envelope with a long list of things to buy: matches, rope, sextants, compass, canvas, sail needles, all the stuff you have to have to buy for a boat."

It was around midnight when we arrived at the farm on October Mountain under a bright, sparkling moon. Arlo, his wife, Jackie, her sister Juanita, and his friend John all greeted us warmly. We were also greeted by their dogs, Eli, Nose, Plunkett, Poppy, and Ginny.

It didn't take long for Jack and Arlo to start talking about old times. Jack mentioned that the other night at the *Gaslight,* a lady had asked him to sing "Goodnight, Little Arlo," one of Woody's songs. He said he hadn't sung it in so long that he didn't know if he knew it anymore.

Then Jack said to Arlo, "I'm gonna play you a tune."

Arlo replied, "I'm gonna play with you." And right away, along with John, they got their guitars out and began picking and singing some fine, homespun tunes. That started off a long spontaneous session of swapping songs. I felt as if I were right on stage with three virtuoso pickers who were each having the time of their lives.

As the night slipped into early morning I observed a special quality in our host. He was authentic, easygoing, and very down-to-earth, the sort of person who, as soon as you meet him, you think you've known forever.

During a break in the singing, I said to Arlo, "You seem content with what you are doing."

He answered sincerely, "Once you stop and say, 'Oh, this is it,' you find yourself in a position that's not all that together. Not when the world needs so much. Not when everybody needs so much."

He paused for a moment, then continued, "All of the things people do are as important as the thing I do. As a musician, anyway, I feel that the object of a musician is to evolve music. The object of a bricklayer is to evolve bricklaying. And that's what really happens. I evolve it with where I'm at. The where-I'm-at-ness is the tool, the means that gets it evolved. But I'm more of a person than a musician. I mean part of me expresses what I am through music, so I have to try to be the best musician I can. I enjoy being what I am. But everybody's got to keep moving. That way, things will happen much more gently."

Satisfied, I went to sleep and didn't wake up until the morning light slipped through the window. After a few sleepy-eyed minutes, I went into the kitchen to find Jackie making pancakes for breakfast.

"It feels real good to be here," I said. "It feels like home."

She stopped stirring the batter for a moment, looked up warmly, and replied, "I'm glad. That's the way it should be."

Then Arlo walked in. "Hi, honey."

"Hi, honey," Jackie returned.

"Morning," he said to me. "How did you sleep?"

"Good morning. Great."

"I have a new song I'd like to sing for you," said Arlo.

He placed a paper with handwritten lyrics on the kitchen table, sat down, and started to sing.

Woke up this morning with my head in my hand.
Come on, children, come on.
The snow was falling all over the land
Come on, children, come on

I don't know, but I been told
Come on, children, come on.
That the streets of heaven have all been sold.
Come on, children, come on.

Come on, children, all come home.
Jesus gonna make you well.
Go to where a man can dwell.

Just then, the overcast sky broke, and a bright ray of sunlight came from behind the clouds, through the window, and right onto the paper he was singing from. Jackie and I looked at each other in amazement as he continued to sing.

Come on, Gabriel, blow that thing
Come on, children, come on
All God's children got to dance and sing
Come on, children, come on

Come on, Gabriel, blow that thing.
Come on, children, come on
All God's children got to dance and sing.
Come on, children, come on

All God's children got to sing and shout,
Come on, children, come on
Ain't nobody round bound to kick you out.
Come on, children, come on

Come on, everybody, what's it worth
Come on, children, come on
To make a heaven out of this earth?
Come on, children, come on

When he concluded, Jackie said, "Honey, that is beautiful."
"It sure is," I added. "And that was quite a confirmation."
"That happened when I wrote the song, too," Arlo declared.

After breakfast we went outside, where the dogs chased anything they could find all over the place and the cats sniffed the fresh air as it blew by. Chickens and goats roamed the yard, ducks swam in the pond, and beyond a nearby stream were green meadows, gently sloping hills, and rugged mountains. We took in the beauty of the landscape as Arlo told us his plans for this newly acquired 250-acre farm.

The chore of the day was to harvest the rocks from the soon-to-be-completed, newly landscaped lawn. We all pitched in, placing the rocks along the edge and building a stone wall fence, while Abe, the Guthries' six-month-old son, watched from his highchair on the porch.

That afternoon Arlo showed us around his land. We made our way along a trail to the top of a gently sloping mountainside. We looked out onto a beautiful valley. To get an even better view, Jack scurried up a pine tree as if he were going aloft on a boat. Arlo and I followed, twisting ourselves around as we climbed, one with the trees.

I reveled in the gift I had been given by this unique individual who had been so open and generous with me. I knew that the land he had taken in trust was in good hands, that the people he would come in contact with would be equally well served.

After dinner, we all sat on the living room floor. Jack played with Aiyana, and Arlo crawled around with Abe, while the dogs rolled around in the middle of it all. Then Jack spotted Arlo's "kid" saddle on a sawhorse, and before we knew it, he had thrown it over his back. Arlo helped him tighten the cinches. Then Aiyana climbed onto the saddle and they cantered around the room.

Jack said, "Now I know what a saddled horse feels like. It's not so bad at all."

I imagined Arlo's childhood in Brooklyn, when Woody must have been doing the same things with *him*. Then I remembered a comment Arlo had made earlier that day: "I don't tend to think of myself as his son, but I do think of him as my father. I'm from there, but not originating from there. I believe that children choose their parents. In order for humankind to continue, one of the things that is absolutely necessary is that we surround ourselves with people who help us evolve to the fullest extent possible, and who help create the circumstances that put us in the position to do the most we can in a lifetime. A lot of people have helped me get to this place. If Woody can dig it, that's fine. I'm sure he can."

I, too, was sure Woody would understand where Arlo was and where he was going. I felt privileged to have this time with Arlo and his family and to have shared with him that sign of acceptance, of confirmation, that had pierced our spirits. I knew that that moment when the sky opened would stay with me, resting deep in my heart, for a long time to come. The storyteller extraordinaire had given me a story to remember, a story to live by.

It was with great reluctance that Jack, Martha, Aiyana, and I left October Mountain the following morning. On the drive back to the city, Martha remarked, "I wish our trip East could have been a little longer."

"We could zigzag," Jack said.

Such is the path of living deliberately, I reflected.

Winter

Back at my cabin by the river, the days grew shorter as the sun's path drew closer to the horizon. Every day the ice on the stream thickened as little waterbeds coalesced into a delicately sculptured frieze.

Soft white flakes, each a separate universe, tumbled through the air in unison, weaving a robe of repose upon the land. Soon even the trees fell asleep.

PURIFICATION

My visit to the Berkshires had inspired me to explore how symbols, myth, and meaning might further enhance my own life. Reflecting on the warm greeting I, a stranger, had received there, the authentic, earthy quality of my hosts, the experience of the sun coming out and shining on Arlo's sheet of song lyrics, and how these linked to my own background in folklore, I knew I had to learn more about how and why the timeless motifs and archetypes that guided the mythic figures of the past came into our lives, as well.

Where do archetypes come from? How and why are they repeated over and over? How and why did the first archetypal experience itself come about? What do the thousands of motifs and archetypes found in the world's sacred literature really mean to us today? Can they be considered universal occurrences? These being the questions of the season, and this a good time to pursue them, I drove down to the city.

That evening, while looking in store windows along 8th Street in Greenwich Village, a book on mythology caught my eye. I went inside the bookshop, quickly found the volume, and began to page through it. Immediately I was engrossed in a captivating theme: the one story that all stories share, the one pattern that all quests follow.

The book, *The Hero with a Thousand Faces,* described the timeless motifs underlying myths of all cultures. Something about this book was familiar, even comforting. Perhaps it was the message that one archetypal pattern bridged past and present, East and West. I knew I wanted to find out more.

Looking up, I noticed a poster announcing a talk on the themes common to all mythologies—and it was being given by Joseph Campbell—the author of the book I was reading! The talk was scheduled for that evening at Cooper Union, only a few blocks away. Glancing at the clock, I saw that I had just enough time to get there.

Without hesitation, I quickly purchased the book and walked over to Cooper Union. I sat down in one of the front rows of the Great Hall and reflected on the passages I had just read about the thousand variations on the one pattern, unaware that the thousand seats around me were filling up.

Soon Joseph Campbell was introduced. He spoke brilliantly, with poise and eloquence, never referring to notes. It felt as if I were the only other person in the room and his words were meant just for me: "The universal formula of the mythological journey is separation, initiation, and return: a hero ventures forth from the world of common day into a region of supernatural wonder; fabulous forces are there encountered and a decisive victory is won; the hero comes back from this mysterious adventure with the power to bestow boons on his fellow men. That is the pattern of the myth, and that is the pattern of the fantasies of the psyche."

What I heard soothed my soul. As he went on, everything he said spoke directly to the experiences I was beginning to become aware of in my own life. Each image he offered was pregnant with a meaning I could feel.

He continued: "All my life, as a student of mythologies, I have been working with the universal archetypes, and I can tell you, they *do* exist and are the same all over the world. The myths and rites will be given different interpretations, different rational applications, different social customs to validate and enforce. And yet the archetypal, essential forms and ideas are the same—often stunningly so. The psychologist who has best described them is Carl G. Jung, who terms them 'archetypes of the collective unconscious,' pertaining to those structures of the psyche that are not the products of merely individual experience but are common to all mankind. . . . The inward journeys of the mythological hero, the shaman, the mystic, and the schizophrenic are in principle the same; and when the return occurs, it is experienced as a rebirth. The new ego lives in accord with society and nature, in harmony, and at peace. The ultimate aim of the quest, if one is to return, must be neither release nor ecstasy for oneself, but the wisdom and power to serve others."

The moments flew by as I took it all in. He spoke a simple, straightforward truth. It confirmed my unexpressed feeling that I was already living parts of the mythic pattern. It *was* comforting to know that such truths arise in the same way for everyone, awakening the same awe and revealing the same mystery.

I reflected on the crossroads I had faced in the bookstore. My choices were: stay where I was, move on to something else, or attend the talk right then. In spontaneously following the instinct that tugged at my heart, in deciding to go hear Joseph Campbell in that moment, I found a sacred realm in the midst of commonplace reality. I became more aware of the power of motifs and archetypes and the meaning and order that they bring to our lives.

The seemingly scattered parts of our lives come together as pieces of some universal puzzle through the organizing message of myth. Our own personal stories and the revelations that emerge from the soul mirror that same truth. In the gift of this understanding, I had found my guide, my teacher, the one to help me recognize the sacred pattern in my own life.

At the end of the talk, I remained seated as most of the crowd disappeared from the hall. A small group of lingering well-wishers had gathered around Campbell at the podium. I knew because of the way his talk had spoken directly to me and my experience that I, too, wanted to say something to him.

I waited a few more minutes to let the crowd thin and to allow my courage to expand. Then I walked up just as the last person was leaving his side.

I cautiously introduced myself and began what I hoped would come out as I wanted, "What you said really meant a great deal to me. In the images you used, and in the pattern you described, I can begin to recognize my own joys and sorrows. I had never imagined that my experiences have been shared by so many others of different times and settings. There must be something very powerful in archetypal images. I feel like I'm in the middle of that pattern right now in my own life. My experiences confirm everything you were saying. I have been helped along too, just as you described in myth, when I needed it most."

"It sounds like you *have* entered the archetypal landscape," Campbell responded. "You should think about how your experience can be shaped and given form that will make it more than just yours."

"I have a lot more to learn about this pattern and how it fits into my life and that of others," I said. "Would it be possible to talk with you more about this sometime?"

"Why, sure," he replied sincerely. He wrote down his address and telephone number, handed me the paper, and said, "Give me a call. We can talk further."

I could tell he was serious, and I was surprised by his openness and his willingness to accommodate me. Was there something in me that he sensed needed encouragement? Did he respond like this to everyone who shows a sincere interest in his passion? On the drive back to the cabin that night, I had much to think about. I wondered where his invitation might lead.

For days afterward, the wailing of the winter wind reminded me of the story of my soul. The wind ripped through the trees, which, though appearing bare, empty, and lonely, were actually staunch in their withdrawal for a season of inner growth. Their leaves, each with its special destiny, had long since found the warm comfort of their source. I, too, yearned for such shelter.

The owner of the cabin had warned me that when winter came I would have to find another place to live. There was no heat in the cabin, and the fireplace was unsafe for regular use. I had to bid my familiar abode farewell and look elsewhere for a dwelling place.

I remembered what a friend had told me about a Franciscan monastery nearby. He thought they took in people who needed a place to stay, primarily the homeless and indigent. It felt like a bad joke at first, but the more I thought about it, the more it seemed like a viable option. Although I didn't qualify as the typical guest, I decided to try it out.

As I arrived at the friary, a silent chill pervaded a gray, unusually somber evening sky. A full moon appeared from behind the clouds, giving a fresh sparkle to the night. Along the winding roadway leading up the mountainside to the inn, the bare arms of the trees were raised in a soliloquy of reverence. The faint silhouette of a solitary friar graced the chapel yard.

Seeking only a bed for the night, I was greeted by a warm embrace of peaceful hospitality. The friar in charge, however, had to ask me the standard questions: Do you have any booze on you? When was the last time you had a drink? How long have you been on the road?

I replied, "I had some orange juice this morning, just before I moved out of my place." I must have answered his questions satisfactorily, as he wrote that my condition upon arrival was "sober" and assigned me to bunk 39. It was about midnight when he showed me into the large, dark, warm dormitory room. All the men there were asleep. I, too, fell quickly asleep.

The next thing I heard was bells—the six o'clock wake-up call. I opened my eyes to a new experience: the bond of mutual caring that emerged from the camaraderie of the men in need. Each man had his own reason for seeking out this shelter. Some were addicts, some could help themselves, others could hardly get out of bed by themselves—all were without a home. No one had to be told when another needed a hand. They sensed it naturally; they knew it from their own experience.

Each assured the other and was of service in some unique way, if simply to show their gratitude for all that had been offered to them. From amid the helpless arose the saintly as the ailing aided the lame.

One older man helped a younger one dress for breakfast, and he returned a gentle, grateful look as best he could. It became evident that within the comfort of unselfish assistance sanctity could be found, and life sustained.

Having been raised in the Protestant faith, I had never imagined myself in a Catholic monastery. When I was in high school, my two closest friends and I used to spend a lot of time talking about religion. One of them was Jewish, and the other Catholic. Our conversations usually ended up with my Jewish friend and me finding some inconsistency in the Catholic religion. But now I could find out for myself what I had thought I knew about this mysterious faith.

Shortly before, I had begun a comparative exploration of other religions and had found a core of spiritual truths common to them all. As a result, religious matters that had previously bothered me no longer seemed important. My hope was to live by the ageless verities of all religions. Here at the friary, I had my opportunity to learn firsthand the truths of a religion I had all but dismissed.

After we all had breakfast, the friars called up the new men—or at least those who could manage it—for their work assignments. Following chores, I asked if I could go see Father Jeremiah, the guardian father of the monastery. The friar said I could.

I walked further up the holy mountain to the cloistered abbey containing Father Jeremiah's office. He greeted me warmly. His office struck me on the one hand as highly unusual for the spiritual leader of the community, yet on the other as most appropriate. The walls were decorated with colorful contemporary posters and banners. One of them read, "Let happiness and peace reign among us all forever."

I explained that I was in between places to live, working on a research project for the sloop restoration. "I was drawn to this sacred fortress in search of understanding," I added.

With grace in his eyes, the guardian father replied, "You are welcome to stay here. In the friary is an empty cell. It shall be yours for as long as you need it."

I was startled by his immediate, unconditional acceptance of me. "Really? I don't know how long I might need a place to stay."

He answered, "Our door is open to you. We give freely that you may find what you seek. In that way, do we all rise to wholeness."

And so I was given refuge in the old friary with a cell to myself. Nestled within a sacred womb, I was free to explore the mysteries of another venerable community. The halls of the monastery buildings were open to me. This was my chance to die to the world, to dwell in an inner sanctuary that nourishes the soul.

With access to the friary, the abbey, the chapel, the shrines, the library, the meeting rooms, the offices, and the large dining room where I could eat with all the brothers, I knew I would be able to explore each of the questions that had already begun filling my mind. That first night in my bare cell, I slept with a sense of freshness, comfort, and anticipation.

Awaking the next morning, I felt another part of me come to life. I swung my legs over the side of the bed and wrote as never before. Thoughts flowed out of me in verse, as drops in a waterfall, and spilled into to my journal:

With our eyes open to the way,
The wonders of the day
Whisper in our ears,
No time for fears.
Seeking joy, playing my part,
I know in my heart
That eternity is ours,
Though we find thorns among flowers.
To each alone, the day unfolds
What the mystery holds.
No more sadness, no more sorrow,
We have seen the light of tomorrow.

It must have been through grace that I felt the heartbeat common to all and began to sense the greater meaning of community. I wrote some more, then left my cell to wander through the friary where all things became new before my eyes.

Outside, past dormant gardens, I observed the brothers at their chores, each with a material as well as spiritual role. The gardener, the baker, the mechanic, and the office worker each served their community in practical ways while also giving counsel and guidance to the visiting laity who came to confide in their word.

That afternoon, I spoke in earnest with Brother Joe, my new brown-robed friend. "What is the meaning of the three knots in the rope belt you wear?" I asked.

"The three knots are for our three vows," I was told. "Poverty, chastity, and obedience."

"They sound like great sacrifices," I noted.

"Our vows draw us toward a higher law. That is where true freedom lies," he assured me.

Through celibacy, could the friar who loves each equally know the love that is most sublime? Could one person's poverty be another's freedom from desire? Could poverty be peace of mind? Could chastity be purity of spirit and, obedience, union with a higher truth?

The following day, my questions focused on the martyr of a thousand ages I saw hanging upon his cross everywhere I wandered. Peering directly into his eyes, I felt his pain in my body; it tore at my soul, as well. How could this be? What is this pain I am feeling? If he is the Son of God, why would he let himself endure such a fate?

This time I confided in Brother Joachim. "Why do we make him look like an albatross?"

"He sacrificed the seed of his life so the tree of his truth might grow," he assured me.

Reaching deep into his heart, he continued, "His sacrifice is the greatest gift of love we have known. No greater love can we comprehend. No greater life can we hope to follow."

After a reflective pause, Brother Joachim added, "There can be no imitation; but since each life has its own burden and its own reward, this love is nearer to you than your own breath."

As I returned to my cell, it sunk in. The love I sought was always within me. But what about hate? Was that always within me, as well? Did I contain *everything* within me? Must I replace animosity with compassion? Letting go of such negativity and unburdened by hate or anger, I could be as water flowing over a rock.

One chilly morning the following week, I took a walk outside the friary and found an iron water tower rising two hundred feet above the mountaintop. Without thinking, I climbed the tower, one thin iron step at a time. At its top, I walked around the platform encircling the water tower and gazed out at the natural beauty and majesty of the Hudson Valley and surrounding mountains.

Amid these thoughts of beauty, I looked down at the land and buildings below and was struck by the possibility of falling to my death. Would I slip? Could I conceivably jump?

Immediately, I understood that my death would have to be accidental. Never would I want to take away my life when there was so much here yet to see and do.

I grasped the cold iron structure more tightly. I was concerned now not so much about death, but about not living fully. When death did come, I knew I wouldn't lose what lasts; I might even gain a great deal more. I only wanted to be able to give the most to each day of the life that I have.

Then another question surfaced: Can I be of any consequence? Up here, not to anyone, but down on the living earth to everyone with whom I can share my truth, was my reply.

I climbed slowly down the steps, and as soon as I touched the earth, I was elated. I headed for the stonewall that circled the friary, sat on its cold surface, and felt an energy warming me from inside.

Then my inner voice returned and spoke clearly: *One yet to know love is as a flower yet to bloom. Let the mysteries of love lead you on.*

Somewhere is a love everlasting and unconditional. Such a love sees with the inner eye and feels with a heart of compassion.

Love's ascent is steep and treacherous. Expect nothing of love except what you give, for love grows not through supremacy but through equality. The servant of this love recognizes in the beloved a sign of the Divine. At its summit, love becomes the intermingling of two souls.

Divine love is the reason for all existence. Not for a moment does it neglect even one life. Love is a circle, and everyone is within its embrace.

As divine love remains constant, so does love's tenderness follow love's patience. Boundless love—a reality for all to know—takes flight from within the open heart, the heart that knows the love of God. Those who see with the eyes of this heart see nothing but love itself.

Back in my cell, I began in earnest my practice of daily prayer and meditation.

CONTINUITY

The weeks passed. One evening as I walked through the monastery halls, a heavenly sound caught my attention. The ethereal music grew fuller, elevating my soul with each step I took toward it.

I was soon in the doorway of the chapel where, from the golden pipes of the organ, a celestial melody swelled, graced by a chorus of chanting friars. I stood transfixed, frozen in time, as the soothing serenade continued. After what seemed like a few hours, I sat in an empty seat in the rear pew and was soon lost in deep meditation as the chanting went on. My mind contemplated the organ music while my soul soared in other realms.

Returning to my cell, I got ready for bed and read from one of my newest books, *The Masks of God: Creative Mythology*. I meditated on the words Joseph Campbell had written upon completing this four-volume enterprise:

I find that its main result for me has been its confirmation of a thought I have long and faithfully entertained:

of the unity of the race of man, not only in its biology but also in its spiritual history, which has everywhere unfolded in the manner of a single symphony, with its themes announced, developed, amplified and turned about, distorted, reasserted, and, today, in a grand *fortissimo* of all sections sounding together, irresistibly advancing to some kind of climax, out of which the next great movement will emerge. And I can see no reason why anyone should suppose that in the future the same motifs already heard will not be sounding still— in new relationships indeed, but ever the same motifs.

I then looked out the window, and my gaze fixed upon a moonlit bare-branched tree with icicle twigs, standing stiff in frozen soil, looming lifeless. Soon afterward, I went to sleep and fell into a dream . . .

My friend Richard and I are walking along a path beside a river in a thickly overgrown forest. We round a bend, whereupon I stop to look at the variety of vegetation. Richard continues along the trail.

Farther upriver, he comes upon a beaver building a dam. Just then, a wolf approaches. To protect the beaver, Richard leans over with a stick, attempting to force the beaver underwater, but Richard falls into the river and he is carried away by the rushing tide.

Sensing that something is wrong, I run on ahead. Finding no sign of Richard on my side of the river, I look across the rushing tide; everything on the opposite side is still and quiet.

Then I lean over to look in the water, when all of a sudden I, too, am pulled into the river, leaving my body behind.

Like a bird whose cage door has been thrown wide open, my spirit takes flight and begins to soar in a limitless sea of light. The water turns to sky. My senses are heightened; my feelings of happiness, more acute.

Then the voice I had become familiar with speaks with conviction:

The horizon of eternity is right before our eyes, for this is a life without end. Think of the leaves that fall and those that follow in the spring, and be assured, life is everlasting.

What is death but life transformed, a passing from one season to the next, for life follows life. And the life that is to come will surely fulfill the life you have known.

Let not the death of those you love pull you closer to your grave. As their energy merges with yours, the life that is theirs becomes a part of you; thus is life carried on into eternity.

When the spirit is freed from the body, its journey is ever-advancing, toward the great reunion. Its progress is dependent upon the grace of God and the prayers of those left behind. Through the love that is passed on continually, all life evolves.

Comfort overcomes me as the light grows brilliant. I want to know its source but, dazed by its splendor, I turn away.

Then I land softly on a verdant meadow. And a great silence falls upon the land. Again I look toward the light.

This time I see seven angels in the distance, each one standing on a stair step ascending a majestic mountain. I sense that Richard is with one of them.

I approach the first angel, who emerges out of the brilliant light, standing upon holy ground, and he invites me toward him.

"I am searching for my friend," I say. "Is he here?"

The angel replies, "I represent an eternal force, having one common womb, mind, and spirit. I bring knowledge of the One Thing out of which all things have sprung. I speak of one law, founded upon wisdom, justice, and equity. Never shall you be left alone. As I am needed, I am born from age to age."

The gate before me opens, the angel vanishes, and I enter, finding a peaceful garden-land where songbirds raise heavenly melodies. But before long, life falls silent. All that had been green is now withered and barren.

After wandering through this wilderness, I eventually see the second angel, bearing in his hand a sparkling staff, and another door to the unknown swings open.

Drawing closer, I see glimpses of an intriguing land beyond. I speak to the angel. "Have you seen my friend? Is he here?"

"As the voice of one angel is hushed in the land, another arises to guide your way. In the beginning, everything was good, yet the path to goodness is strewn with many temptations. Follow this path with purity, help others along this path, and you shall surely attain your goal. This is our promise, our everlasting covenant."

The second gate opens, the angel vanishes, and I am ushered into a land of justice and truth. After a while, however, the inhabitants of this land forget the words of the angel and become defiled and aimless. Simultaneously, the landscape turns dark and arid. But again a light shines from the mountaintop to guide my path.

The third angel then appears, bowing with hands together. I approach and say, "I don't understand. I am only looking for my friend, and instead I find words of wisdom."

The angel replies, "Happy is the one who enters, by way of restraint, giving, and undivided love, the abodes of the soul.

Revere the earth, make sacred your work, and value all of the peoples of humanity. We are the birthless, the deathless. Common be our intention, perfect is our unity."

Then the angel steps aside, and the gate to another realm opens. Before me lies a land of promise, where songs of praise abound. Yet in time, the people follow their own ways, and as earlier, the spirit of life is lost.

Continuing on my quest, I see the fourth angel, a perfect mirror of light, carrying three baskets. Here I sense a new element to my nature. I realize I had not only been hearing what the angels were saying but attempting to incorporate their words into my spirit.

"In my search for my friend, I am finding my own inner harmony. Why is that?" I ask.

The angel answers, "As you have seen, I am not the first like myself, nor shall I be the last. We are called the enlightened ones. We have each provided a portion of the guidance you need to progress in your journey. Be patient, as you tread the middle path you shall become a lamp unto others, leading the way to universal fellowship."

The gate of this land opens wide, and as the angel vanishes, I walk into a noble, resplendent realm, where truth reigns supreme. But before long, the light dims and all forms of life wither and pale.

A star falls from the sky, and the fifth angel appears, who heralds a vibrant domain. A breeze of contentment blows over me. This time I am silent for want of fitting words.

The angel speaks saying, "Love all who come your way, even as yourself, and great shall be your reward. Walk in the light; let not your heart be troubled. Much more is there to say, but now is not the time. I will return to you again."

The gate to this land opens, and I step into a borderless city teeming with happiness. Yet before long, veils of misunderstanding divide the people and they lose their joy.

Soon the sixth angel emerges from a barren, rocky desert, with peace upon his brow.

"I have noticed a common thread running through the words of the angels," I say.

The angel assures me, "We appear in time of need to confirm the pillars of tradition. No difference do we make between any of us. We are each light upon light. Guided is the one who is submissive. Indeed, you are already on your journey back from where you have come."

Then he ushers me into the precincts of a holy region replete with fragrant gardens of delight beside shimmering streams. Again the people begin to interpret for themselves and fall into discord. I move on, certain I would find the seventh angel.

Hearing a refreshing chant coming from what I think is a heavenly abode, I am drawn instead to a dark, deplorable prison cell. Here many who sought an everlasting truth huddle together about one with a radiant countenance. Though mired in filth and weighed down with chains, they beam with light and joy and beckon me to join them.

I hesitate but then realize that this must be the abode of the seventh angel. I step in and am warmly welcomed.

An expectant hush falls over the cell. The angel, holding an open book, says, "This is an ancient, universal, and ever-unfolding faith that we all herald. We clear the path of impediments to your progress. Each angel is from the one source, as rays of one light. Every time one of us appears, it is to build anew the whole world."

The voice of the seventh angel resounds with clarity, and I feel the quickening breeze of life pour over me like a mighty torrent. I take in every syllable as he continues. "A spiritual springtime has arrived. This is the day of promise. This is the time for a world-embracing vision. Dedicate yourself to the service of the entire human family and to the advancement of civilization."

Serenity swells up within me as the gentle tones of the angel's voice gives me the courage to commit to carrying out my responsibility.

The cell transforms into a mountainside of aromatic gardens with beds of flowers and rows of cypress trees. A murmuring stream flows beside them fringed with willows; the air, fragrant with scents of jasmine and orange; and in the distance, even the desert blooms. Below, a harbor sparkles with the shimmering lights of ships bearing pilgrims from all over the globe.

Upon the mountainside surrounding me are majestic shrines. Circling them are people from every corner of the globe, and of every hue, raising songs of joy. From all sides of the mountain, melodious voices sound their praise at daybreak.

RENEWAL

As I awoke the following morning, I opened my eyes slowly, for I sensed a different world around me. At first I could not recognize my monastic cell, nor did I remember going to sleep there the night before.

The bitter cold of the morning, however, snapped me back to reality. Tiny ice crystals on the window blocked my view of the grounds outside, but resting my arms upon the sill and taking a closer look, I could see a layer of frost covering the field below. Off to the right was the same bare-branched tree I'd seen the night before, erect in the frozen soil.

The barrenness of the tree brought me back to my dream, which was still clear in my mind. But what was its meaning? What was my dream really trying to tell me?

As I reflected further, especially on the seven angels, I was drawn to the book by my bedside, *The Bible of the World*, containing, all in one volume, the profound and beautiful scriptural essence of all religious traditions.

I opened the book to a page where a scholar was quoted as saying: "There is but one religion for humanity; the many faiths and creeds are all streams or streamlets of this great river. . . . The Sun of Truth is one. His rays stream forth into the minds and hearts of men." Then the words of Paul, in his Epistle to the Ephesians, made even more sense: "There is one body, and one spirit . . . one Lord, one faith, one baptism, one God and Father of all, who is above all, and through all, and in you all." This, I realized, is exactly what my dream was telling me.

From the Upanishads, I read, "How many gods are there really?" "One," was the reply. And from the Bhagavad-Gita, "The Blessed Lord said: 'By me all this world is pervaded in My Unmanifested aspect; all beings have root in me. . . . The same am I to all beings.'"

From the Book of Isaiah, I read, "I am the Lord, and there is none else, there is no God besides me." And from the Zendavesta, "Then Zarathustra said: 'Reveal unto me that name of thine, O Ahura Mazda, that is the greatest, the best, the fairest.' . . . Ahura Mazda replied unto him: 'My name is the One of whom questions are asked.'"

From the Buddhist scriptures, I read, "Great Being! There is none your equal, much less your superior." From the Gospel of Mark, "The Lord our God is one Lord." And from the Koran, "He is God, the One and Only; God the Eternal, Absolute . . . and there is none like unto Him."

Then I reached for another well-used book from my shelf, *The Religions of Man.* Huston Smith also provided a clear sense of the big picture: "Authentic religion is the clearest opening through which the inexhaustible energies of the cosmos can pour into human existence. . . . Perhaps we are able to see man's religions more as faiths of real people, people who are asking the same basic questions that we are, seekers like us of the illumined life."

He then asks the all important question: how do these religions fit together? He offers three possible answers: either, a) one of the religions of man stands "so incomparably superior that no significant religious truth is to be found in any of the others which is not present in equal or clearer form within this religion itself" or, b) "in all important respects they are the same," each containing "some version of the Golden Rule," and each acknowledging "a universal Divine Ground from which man has sprung " or, c) all religions are not saying the same things, though their "unity is in certain respects both striking and impressive. But neither, in the presence of differences, does it assume that all important truths can be found in any single tradition."

Leaving the answer to this dilemma of overall fit to personal reason, he suggests that we learn to listen to the faiths of others. This caused me to wonder further why we tend to think more in narrow, limited contexts when we can just as easily think in terms of the inclusive whole of which they are all part.

What struck me now was how much clearer it seemed that there were a myriad paths leading from a single sacred origin, that there was a timeless thread connecting each of the paths, that each path led back to the same source— that therefore an underlying unity connected all of the divinely inspired traditions. I realized that I had a responsibility to focus my own search for truth on such wholeness.

As I thought more about these sacred traditions, each one having a founder entrusted with a special message, I remembered a brochure I had picked up at one of the sloop festivals during the summer describing the principle of "progressive revelation."

I went to find this brochure, which was tucked away in one of my books on mythology. The brochure explained how it is as if the Creator has sent His messengers, His mirrors, to reflect a heavenly light toward earth, each coming at a different time and place, when and where most needed, to add another chapter to the endless Book of God.

Each prophet, from ancient times to the present, has a common purpose in the same universal, continuous, unfolding evolutionary process, periodically reconnecting the world to the realm of the spirit. Each one has its essential role in furthering the evolution of our spiritual and social consciousness.

The brochure said the most recent Messenger in this long line of prophets, Bahá'u'lláh, had come not only to reconfirm that spiritual truth is one, but to affirm that humanity is one, that the diverse peoples of the world make up but one race, the human race, and that humanity stands at the threshold of an era that will transform its moral and spiritual life. It said the teachings of Bahá'u'lláh, the Founder of the Bahá'í Faith, were a ringing call to action, offering hope, courage, and vision to peoples of all ethnic and religious backgrounds throughout the world.

In His own words, Bahá'u'lláh confirmed what I had been surmising: "This is the changeless Faith of God, eternal in the past, eternal in the future." I could clearly recognize now a process that had begun millennia ago and has today reached a critical juncture. Humanity stood at a spiritual and social crossroads; yet I also felt assured that, with our own commitments and actions, this process will continue forever onward, to a culmination we can only vaguely imagine today.

This all made much more sense now. If there is only one Creator of the universe, why would He not send multiple messengers throughout our long history, each to reveal a portion of an unfolding truth, each a reminder of divine unity, each one to guide a fragmented humanity toward its oneness and beyond, toward the realization of the long-awaited and shared vision of unity, peace, and lasting harmony?

And in such a case, not only do the peoples of the world have more in common than we think, we have even more to say to each other, and more to learn from each other, about our spiritual heritage and our destiny.

Could it be that our greatest gift to one another is simply to listen deeply, with open hearts, to the stories of faith we each carry?

I turned my gaze out the window and saw the cold pallor of the winter landscape transform in full-blown animation. The roots of the dormant tree stirred beneath the hardened soil, pushing a new life force up into its frozen limbs. Fresh buds appeared, leaves unfurled, and the boughs turned verdant again.

I then felt a new life force growing within *me*. Odd as it seemed, the presence of my grandmother became so strong that I sensed she wanted to tell me something important. Could it be that she had been with me every step of the way? Was she helping me make sense of the unknown? Just as she silently guided me in life, maybe she was continuing to guide me even now. Life and death could be one indivisible reality between which consciousness can flow as freely as the wind, I thought.

Once more I heard the voice I had come to believe in:

As you face your challenges in life, remember to be loving, gentle, and respectful in every circumstance; remember that life is a recurring cycle of crises and triumphs, both necessary parts of the whole. Love is the mystery that unites opposites, transforming sorrow into joy. I will be with you always. Yet you are your own guide, too. You have been a good listener; now listen to the truth of others, for in listening well you give your love.

As I looked up again, the tree became the center of a bountiful garden, transporting me back to the paradise of my dream. And I thought that maybe it had been with my grandmother's help that I had made my way through the dreamscape, too.

My task became even clearer: to live lovingly and greet all that comes my way with grateful appreciation. With this as my focus, I will be able to offer a steady hand in the circle of humanity.

As the days passed, my thoughts at the monastery came relentlessly back to the promise of the vision that had sprung to life that bitter morning. But how, exactly, would my task be carried out in the world? What role would I slip into that is meant just for me in this world? I became all the more ready to find it.

Finally, one Sunday, I could wait no longer within the cloistered walls of the monastery. The ice and the snow had long since melted. The brook beside the abbey swelled as it rushed by. Daffodils brightened the fields, and the sun was higher than it had been for months.

I made my way through the long narrow halls to the guardian father's inner chamber. I paused a moment and then knocked.

I was ushered inside, and with gratitude for the guardian father and the friars seated there, I explained: "I found my way to your sanctuary from another tradition. I had no intention to wear the robe or take on the vows. I wanted only to live more deeply and see if I could experience a spiritual life. Yet you gave me shelter and more. You even referred to me as the 'unfrocked friar.' This is indeed a blessed spot, and I found more here than I could have imagined. I have uncovered the roots of my destiny. I am grateful to have shared your home. Now I must reenter the mainstream of life."

The guardian father, moved by my heartfelt affirmation, stood and approached me, extending his arms. After embracing me in a spirit of brotherhood, he whispered in my ear, "Spread your joy around the world."

Brother Joe and the others wished me well, too. The next morning, I loaded my meager belongings into my red VW and drove down the holy mountain.

Spring

Nature was shaking off its long rest. Songbirds struck up a symphony. Newly arrived flower buds dotted the bare twigs of the tulip trees. Wild berries began to claim their color. Raindrops lingered on pine needles.

The Hudson itself was vibrant with runoff from the mountains. Everywhere, the fragrance of seedtime announced a season of fresh growth. And a gentle breeze nudged my soul.

RETURN

I drove toward New York City without knowing exactly where I would end up. As I thought about my options, it seemed like a perfect time to visit Joseph Campbell, if he was available. I called him; he remembered me and was able to see me at four o'clock.

I arrived at his home in Greenwich Village, and he greeted me as warmly as he had the first time we met. He invited me up, introduced me to his wife, Jean, and showed me into the den, where we sat down and talked. I told him, in more detail, how my adventures seemed to have led me from one archetypal opportunity to another.

"That is similar to my own adventure when I was 'on the road' around your age," he said.

We spoke for what seemed like hours about how life mirrors myth. His enthusiasm and vitality were beyond any I had experienced, as was his understanding of life's sacred themes.

As our time together came to a close, he said to me, "The archetypes in your experience represent your most reliable truth. Integrate them into your everyday living. Transmit their meaning to others."

I expressed my deep gratitude to him for sharing his insights with me, for showing such regard for my life and its possibilities, and for the practical knowledge his life-long study of mythology had brought me and so many others.

On my way to the car, I remembered solitude has its season, but the decree of spring is fellowship. I got in my car and headed eastward, eager to see my old friends and tell them of all that had happened to me.

Once on the expressway, new questions arose: Who, having seen a boundless world, would return to the old? The world I had called "home" was as different from the one I now knew as heaven is from earth. Who would believe what I had seen? Who would understand what I had to say?

Torn between two realities, I recalled Richard's words just before we left the summer camp: "Greatest is the dream that awakens those of others."

Right away, the power of my own vision returned, as strong as it had been when I first felt it in my heart. I realized more fully that the realm of mysterious wonder is but a deeper layer of everyday reality.

I understood that we are not only free to pass back and forth between the two realities but *must* do so in order to plant seeds of understanding in the garden of the spirit. For in reality the two are one. It was then that the parting words of Joseph Campbell took on even deeper significance.

Without further delay I continued on, desiring first to return to the familiar shore, lined with fresh dune grass, and immerse my toes in the soft sands of the isle of my birth. The moment I saw the sparkling waves and darted in and out of their sea spray, pearls of assurance washed upon me, bringing joy to my heart. The feeling of being home again was greatly welcomed.

The next morning, I stopped by my alma mater, the college with its windmill on the hill. While walking through the hallway of the new humanities building, I came upon one of my favorite professors.

"I *thought* that was you," he said. "What have you been up to?"

I explained all that I had been doing, and he brought me up to date on the changes that had taken place in the three years since I had graduated.

He went on to say, "This is good timing. We're offering a course this term called 'Contemporary Folk-Rock Lyrics as Poetry,' but the instructor just decided to spend the time working on his dissertation instead."

"Really? That's a topic I've become very interested in," I said. "I've recently found many timeless themes in today's folk-rock lyrics."

"Maybe you could help us out. Would you consider teaching the course?"

"Oh, I'd love to!" I said instinctively, without fully knowing what I would encounter.

Later that day, after my appointment was made official, I had second thoughts. I wasn't sure I was ready to take on this opportunity. It would be my first teaching experience.

Would I have enough time to prepare? Would I know what to say? Would I be able to say what I wanted to?

In the end, I had to admit that, although being a teacher would challenge the image I had of myself, it could fulfill my desire to assist others in reaching their potential. Maybe it would even help *me* leave my childhood silence behind.

I settled into my decision and went right to work fleshing out the syllabus, getting the lyrics together, and thinking about the context within which I wanted to present them.

We would trace the development of the music and culture that had become known as folk-rock; we would consider representative lyrics for their aesthetic appeal, their philosophical value, and their historical and contemporary meaning; and we would discuss, from a mythological perspective, the themes that emerged. Some of the songwriters to be studied would be Bob Dylan, Arlo Guthrie, Joni Mitchell, James Taylor, Carol King, Paul Simon, Cat Stevens, and Laura Nyro.

But I also knew I needed to explore much more what teaching and learning meant to me and how I could best facilitate that vital process.

First, I remembered Plato's allegory of the cave, in which the shadows on the wall are taken for reality from the limited perspective of the cave dwellers, because what is visible in the cave represents all of what is known to them. Yet there is much more than this. Emerging from the cave and entering a new world beyond, new understandings become possible, and the shadows are recognized for what they are—illusion. In education, with many levels of understanding possible, we could either be satisfied with what is apparent or look deeper for what is not apparent. In applying my study of philosophy, I wanted the practice of reflection to inform my teaching.

For Plato, education was not a process of filling empty minds with what they don't know, but one of leading receptive minds to recognize what they already know. And I thought that if I could help guide my students beyond what is familiar to them, beyond the mere shadows of the cave wall, and lead them out into the openness of a new expanse where previously invisible truths lay, I might be able to assist them into the light of their own lives, and I, too, would be rewarded.

Next I thought of Confucius and *The Great Learning,* in which he speaks about the education of the "superior man" being the pursuit of illustrious virtue. Yet, again, the paradox is that the qualities resulting in the highest personal and social ethic are innate within. The way of the superior man leads to harmony between heaven, man, and earth. In one thus educated, "all things are nourished together without their injuring one another . . . all-embracing and vast, is he like heaven." This, indeed, would be a most worthy outcome for a course on any subject.

Emerson again came to my mind. His talk at Cambridge on the American scholar offered me much at this moment. He envisioned an inclusive and lifelong context for learning: "Is not, indeed, every man a student, and do not all things exist for the student's behoof?" This, I thought, was at least the baseline that needed to be considered in every classroom.

His mention of nature as the first in importance of the influences in the education of the scholar was particularly intriguing to me:

Every day, the sun; and, after sunset, night and her stars. Ever the winds blow; ever the grass grows. Every day, men and women, conversing, beholding and beholden. The scholar is he of all men whom this spectacle most engages. He must settle its value in his mind. What is nature to him? There is never a beginning, there is never an end, to the inexplicable continuity of this web of God, but always circular power returning into itself. Therein it resembles his own spirit, whose beginning, whose ending, he never can find,—so entire, so boundless. . . .

Thus to him, to this school-boy under the bending dome of day, is suggested, that he and it proceed from one root; one is leaf and one is flower; relation, sympathy, stirring in every vein. And what is that Root? Is not that the soul of his soul?—A thought too bold,—a dream too wild. Yet when . . . he has learned to . . . see that the natural philosophy that now is, is only the first gropings of its gigantic hand, he shall look forward to an ever-expanding knowledge as to a becoming creator.

Emerson knew, too, how this influence impacts the overall purpose of "higher" education. "Colleges . . . can only highly serve us," he said, "when they aim not to drill, but to create; when they gather from far every ray of various genius to their hospitable halls, and, by the concentrated fires, set the hearts of their youth on flame."

In another of his essays, Emerson wrote: "There is no teaching until the pupil is brought into the same state or principle in which you are; a transfusion takes place; he is you and you are he." In Emerson's musings, I had clearly found my greatest challenge as a new teacher.

Then I remembered *Black Elk Speaks,* and I wondered if a classroom experience could come anywhere close to re-creating the wonder and mystery of being in the heart of nature and hearing a voice meant just for oneself, as Black Elk had heard: "Behold a sacred voice is calling you; all over the sky a sacred voice is calling." I thought that this kind of experience, wherever it might happen, is like hearing one's inner voice, the voice that lifts one to the heights of understanding.

And I also thought of Black Elk's vision, which he received at the age of nine, perhaps because he had already been prepared to receive whatever was waiting for him to see beyond what he was familiar with. I felt that the gift of such a vision is that it brought him as much into the present moment as possible while also deeply connecting him to the entire creation.

Then a Voice said: "Behold this day, for it is yours to make. Now you shall stand upon the center of the earth to see, for there they are taking you." . . . Then I was standing on the highest mountain of them all, and round about beneath me was the whole hoop of the world. And while I stood there I saw more than I can tell and I understood more than I saw; for I was seeing in a sacred manner the shapes of all things in the spirit, and the shape of all shapes as they must live together like one being. And I saw that the sacred hoop of my people was one of many hoops that made one circle."

I wondered if wanting to have a role in trying to facilitate a kind of holistic learning were too great a challenge to even consider. Perhaps I *could* strive to help my students see more than they can tell and understand more than they saw; then might they be able to recognize the one circle we and all else are part of.

It was now clear to me that my philosophy of teaching and learning reflected who I was; it came directly from my own life experience and from the influences that had had the greatest impact on me. This was what I knew best. This was what had worked well for me. And this was what I could best pass on to others.

I wanted most to engage my students in an ongoing process of reflection, to give them the opportunity to become fully absorbed in a topic, and to encourage them to share their reflective thoughts so we could learn from each other what our deepest motivations and convictions are.

If this collaborative effort worked well, if we all shared our discoveries and our biggest questions, we would become a community learning as much from ourselves and each other as from any textbook. And in so doing, we might tap into the reservoir of the spirit.

My hope was that I could convey what I had discovered to others, create a setting within which a reflective approach could have relevance for others, and inspire their own creative thinking.

By the time the class was to start, I felt as ready as I could be to take on my newest challenge.

GRATITUDE

On the first day of class, we sat in a circle and I looked into the faces of my students, one by one.

I spoke freely and truthfully; words poured forth, as if flowing from my soul: "My job, as teacher, is to help you uncover the wisdom already within you. Your job, as learner, is to be open to your own mysteries. My challenge is to facilitate this process; yours is to seek the meaning that makes the whole greater than any of its parts.

"What is learning if not uncovering the secrets buried within? Are we not learning every second we are conscious of the lives we are living? Our greatest wisdom comes from the vast expanse within us. Everything we learn reveals the beginning of something more to be learned. Your own experience—and the understanding you gain from that—is the source of your greatest learning.

"Like the gardener who carefully prunes his plants, I would remove what is in your way. I would guide you beyond the surface of your mind, and past the walls of your daily routine, to the deeper meaning of your life.

"Something within us all lies untapped until we let go of whatever we think we need to hold on to. Our detachment from the material world lifts us into a greater awareness of life's boundlessness, timelessness, and sacredness. In this realm, we bring into being the realization of our own potential.

"Open your eyes to the moment, grasp the wonder of its existence. Everything, big and small, is a clue, each important in its own way. As the morning glory's moment of brightness can be an eternity, so can a moment of quiet deliberation serve you for a lifetime.

"The universe is our classroom. Everything we need to know is unfolding all around us. Within the workings of nature are revealed divine lessons with each passing season. Let your curiosity lead you further and further into life's mysteries. The education that matters the most, and prepares us for a life of learning, is that which connects us with our own spirit."

I took a deep breath as I looked around at the students again. They had been listening intently. We went on to introduce ourselves, and then to an overview of the course and syllabus.

As that first class came to a close, I realized that I could trust myself, that I could speak for myself, that others would listen to what I said, and that, for the first time, I had been speaking with my inner voice; I wanted only to be able to call upon it whenever I needed it. I imagined it as the voice of love, my greatest ally.

Beginning with the next class, as we engaged in discussions of the meaning of many contemporary folk-rock lyrics, especially how the songs follow the mythological journey of separation, initiation, and return, the students and I became better acquainted. A couple of them remembered me from when I was a student at the college.

The first song we listened to, a song expressing the archetype of separation, was Arlo Guthrie's "Highway in the Wind." I passed out the lyrics so we could follow the words along with the song.

Sail with me into the unknown void
That has no end,
Swept along the open road
That don't seem to begin.
Come with me and love me, Babe,
I may be back again.
Meantime I'll keep sailing down
This highway in the wind . . .

The fortune-teller tells me
I have somewhere to go.
I look and try to understand
And wonder how she knows.
So I must be going now,
I'm losing time my friend,
Looking for a rainbow
Down this highway in the wind.

The first response from a student was, "When you really listen to the words, the song sounds even better. It makes even more sense. But is it poetry?"

I tossed the question back to them, "What do you think? Looking at the song lyric as bare lines of words, with nowhere to hide on the printed page, is a tough test for any songwriter to pass. What *does* make a lyric a poem?"

One student said, "It rhymes, it has verses, and it seems to have meter."

"It expresses experiences, feelings, and emotions," said another.

"It seems different than regular speech. It seems to carry more power, too."

"And, it uses words, images, and ideas that many people can relate to, and maybe even understand from their own experience," noted another student.

"Very good," I commented. "Sometimes a song can say strikingly sensitive and penetrating things that most everyday conversation can't even touch. There are images, metaphors, and meanings in Arlo's song that do seem to stay with you. It may be that one of poetry's greatest contributions is to be able to pass timeless meaning across very different times. Arlo seems to be echoing the experience and sentiment of Walt Whitman, who wrote:

Afoot and lighthearted I take to the open road,
Healthy, free the world before me,
The long brown path before me leading wherever I choose.

Henceforth I ask not good-fortune—I myself am good-fortune.

"And Whitman may be echoing William Blake, who was echoing Dante, who in turn echoed Homer. Times change, but life's most important issues remain constant."

Then we listened to a few more songs on this theme, Joni Mitchell's "Urge for Going," James Taylor's "Country Road," Cat Stevens's "Father and Son," and others.

The students quickly became adept at recognizing the timeless motifs in the songs. One asked, "How can there be so many different experiences and situations to express the same theme?"

I tried to explain, "We're just beginning to look at songs that mirror a timeless pattern. Identifying the elements of this pattern will become even clearer as we go on. These songwriters are speaking from their own experience, and their sentiments are real. But they speak of life as it has always been and always will be. Their poetry represents not only our age, but also the archetypal experiences played out for millennia.

"What we have heard so far represents the first phase of the mythological journey, the archetype of the 'call to adventure,' when we leave the familiar behind and enter a new realm. As Joseph Campbell says, experiencing this archetype 'signifies that destiny has summoned the hero and transferred his spiritual center of gravity from within the pale of society to a zone unknown.' There are many ways this 'fateful region' can be represented, in every corner of the world, but all are expressions of an independent search through which we find our own truth."

In the next class, we listened to songs of initiation. First in this group was Laura Nyro's "Time and Love."

So winter froze the river
And winter birds don't sing
Winter makes you shiver
So time is gonna bring you spring

He swears he'll never marry
Says that cuddles are a curse
Just tell him plain
You're on the next train

If love don't get there first
Time and love, everybody, time and love
Nothing cures like time and love

So Jesus was an angel
And mankind broke His wing
But Jesus gave His lifeline
So sacred bells could sing

Now a woman is a fighter
Gathered white or African
A woman is a woman, inside
Has riches for her man

Time and love
Nothing cures like time and love.

The first student responding said, "This makes it clear that we always face challenges. But it is hopeful, too, in that we can overcome them in time."

Another said, "It also seems to say that giving in to temptations can be a real challenge. But if we just wait a moment the next thing may be better for us."

And a very perceptive student pointed out, "This song is very relevant to our time because it brings in the contributions of women; they are at least equal to those of men. And not only that, it values all people in the same way."

"What I like," said another, "is how it's not only time that heals, but love, too."

"You have all made important points here," I added. "Life is an ongoing initiation, and each situation we find ourselves in is really meant to assist our progress. Most of the challenges we face are inner struggles. There *is* built-in hope in the mythological journey of the hero, but we need something to guide us through the challenges and temptations, like a clear standard or set of personal values.

"Joseph Campbell said that 'woman, in the language of mythology, represents the totality of what can be known.' Maybe women's rights, along with civil rights, have finally found their time to be fully understood and brought into being. Related to this is that the boon itself to be gained from the arduous mythological journey is a love that is boundless. This realization goes a long way in bringing about the renewal and rebirth central to the journey."

We went on in another class to consider the lyrics of songs of return. Here we listened to the Moody Blues' "The Balance."

After he had journeyed,
And his feet were sore,
And he was tired,
He came upon an orange grove
And he rested
And he lay in the cool,
And while he rested, he took to himself an orange and
    tasted it,

And it was good.
And he felt the earth to his spine,
And he asked, and he saw the tree above him, and the
    stars,
And the veins in the leaf,
And the light, and the balance.
And he saw magnificent perfection,
Whereon he thought of himself in balance,
And he knew he was.

Just open your eyes,
And realize, the way it's always been. . . .

And he thought of those he angered,
For he was not a violent man . . . ,
And he understood. . . .
And he learned compassion.

And with his eye of compassion
He saw his enemies like unto himself,
And he learned love.
Then, he was answered.

We pondered the printed lyrics a moment more. "This kind of understanding seems like it would take a lot of work," one student offered. "When the journey is completed it's not really over, it requires deep, thoughtful reflection."

"And probably many questions, too, about what it all means," said another.

"Sometimes, momentarily, I might be able to see 'magnificent perfection,' in nature, especially, but to be able to see this in myself, or to see myself in balance, that seems like quite a stretch," another student revealed.

A student added, "I wonder if balance on the personal level leads to balance on the social level. This song may even be saying something about balance between social and economic extremes, too."

"I can see this song having implications beyond the personal, too," another said. "The '60s *were* a time of extremes, with the pendulum swinging from one side to the other so often and so quickly. All we could have asked for was a balance between the two."

"Yes, I think that's it," said another. "It was all so turbulent and chaotic, too much, too fast. If it had all happened slower, we might have felt the balance more."

"It seems to follow, if more people find this inner balance, it would add to the balance in society," another commented.

"I can relate to the difficulty of seeing this balance in myself, not to mention society," said another student.

And another added, "This balance the song speaks of is really some kind of middle ground between heaven and earth, very difficult to find, much less maintain."

"I think you are all identifying the reality of this part of the journey very well," I said. "It is not easy for the adventurer to return with a gift that is understood or readily received by others. This may be the greatest challenge of the journey that never ends. If, and when, we come to this understanding, what do we do with what we have been given?

"First is to accept the responsibility that comes with the understanding. But our survival at this point depends upon the realization that the two kingdoms are actually one—different parts of the same whole, and that if we live consciously with the understanding we have been given, if our gift is given without expectation, and if we accept whatever our place in the world is, we will be able to move freely back and forth between the two realms and be grateful for our life."

Then I added, "Even, or maybe especially, during a time when a war in a far away country demands much of our thoughts, as these songwriters have shown us, we still have our own lives to live. We still have to figure out what they mean for us."

After considering a few more lyrics in this vein, like Cat Stevens's "On the Road to Find Out," Bob Dylan's "New Morning," and James Taylor's "Lo and Behold," our heartfelt discussions had brought us together as mentors to each other, learning together from the themes and issues in the songs. And the course became like a workshop where everyone expressed what was foremost on their minds.

In the next to last class, while in our circle, a student took the entire course to its most practical level, asking sincerely, "What we have talked about here has been stimulating, but what can we *do* with it? How can we *use* it?"

I replied, "When you find a song, a poem, or anything else, which speaks directly to you, you have found the essence of your own life, an answer to one of your own unasked questions. Find something in the journey of another similar to that of your own, and you will realize you are living the journey of the soul.

"The timeless truth of myth is being carried out each day of our lives. These songwriters express a current mythology in the language of today, created from real experiences of chaos and despair, love and beauty. This new mythology relates not to a wilting past, but to a planet of conquered horizons.

"Each one of us has experiences that connect us to others. This is the usefulness, the lesson, within the archetypes of myth. As we respond to their living truth with belief and lasting commitment, we are introduced to our universal self, the hero or heroine of our own adventure. And it is this understanding that may become the most practical of all learning as we carry out our lives in conscious relationship to others."

I paused for a moment, wanting to see if they were still with me. It seemed like they wanted to hear more, so I went on, speaking from my own experience. "You have a choice in all your actions. The decisions you make determine your destiny. Each day as you strive to bring forth your inner virtues, your inner goodness, your own divinity will emerge. The greatest need in the world today is for each of us to know intimately our own spiritual nature, to live into our spiritual calling."

Then a student who had not yet spoken stopped me and said, "Spiritual seems to be one of those words that can have many meanings. What do you mean by that?"

"Yes, this is a term, like many, shrouded in mystery, but spirituality has a long history in this country, and beyond. The Transcendentalists understood spirituality as our deepest interior cravings, what we all aspire to; as the poetry of the soul, expressed with an energy that connects us to the divine; as a contemplative stillness, allowing a freedom of insight; as a religion of the spirit.

"Yet living a spiritual life is totally subjective. It is doing what matters most to you, it is being aware of what you most passionately love, it is carrying out a deep respect for the mysteries of life; it is doing what is personally sacred to you. It is knowing what draws you to and connects you with all of life.

"As you come to know your sacred self, a longing will grow within you, all separation will vanish, and you will find yourself deeply connected with all life around you. Your true calling is to valiant acts of service. All your endeavors can be as a prayer, if carried out with the intent to increase the visibility of love in the world."

And another student asked, "But how can we know our true calling when those closest to us have other plans in store for us?"

This question had flowed as naturally as what had preceded it, and I knew this was the opportunity everything in the course had been leading up to. "Before it is too late," I answered, "get to know those who have given you life. This will help you discover your own uniqueness. It is out of your parents' union that you have come forth to find the union within your own self. If you follow your own heartbeat, you will encounter the hurdles meant to ultimately propel you to your own fulfillment.

"By adhering to your own internal integrity, whatever work you do can become worship. The work most fulfilling is that which contributes to justice among the peoples of the world; the work most comforting brings one soul into communion with another.

"When you are in touch with your true nature, you are able to know gratitude for all the gifts received, even those not wanted. Gratefulness comes with giving up control of what is beyond your control. Regardless of what you have been given, your greatest gift to those who have given you life may be forgiveness for what they were unable to give you.

"As the tide returns to the shore, so do we, each in our own time, return with greater love for the source of our being. In this way, you become a blossom of their spirit. You may even find your greatest reward someday in the children of *your* spirit."

"You were a student here just a short time ago," said one who had known me before. "How have you arrived at such understandings?"

I felt I needed to respond to this honest query by explaining even more fully my own experience. "It is not always, or even necessarily, the passage of time, or age, that brings such understandings, but, even more so, our own deep reflection on the experiences we do have. I have been to places that seemed to be waiting for me to arrive. I have come full circle, returning to where I began my journey, yet nothing appears quite the same as it did before.

"My own understandings of the experiences I have had have added depth to my soul only because I became aware of what was happening to me as it happened. I took time to let each experience sink deep within me and become a vital part of me. I looked for hidden dimensions in the clear-cut. My experiences became most useful to me when I was able to recognize how they connect me to everyone else.

"When I discovered that the mythic pattern was what I was living, through reading what I was most deeply drawn to, and through being guided by a mentor who had discerned this pattern in his own life and in the lives of the classic heroes and heroines, I saw with different eyes.

"Now I see the whole before the parts, the universal before the particular, and the perennial before the changing. Might this understanding be available to us all, as we seek to recognize the underlying spiritual laws of the universe?

"It seems that every generation has found this in their own way. Emerson, with his idea of the one soul that links us all, along with Thoreau and Whitman, spoke with this consciousness in the last century. Before them, the purpose of all the great prophets of all the great sacred traditions has been to explain what is beyond our physical world and what the patterns are that uphold this transcendent reality. Joseph Campbell, Carl Jung, and others speak of the universal spiritual realm today.

"In our own generation, many of the songwriters we have listened to seem to express this understanding. We are the first generation to see our wholeness reflected back to us from the moon. It is our challenge now to have what is not readily visible at a quick glance become, through deep reflection, the obvious.

"The meaning I have found upon my path is very personal, yet at the same time something you may know directly. Perhaps my experience is a mirror of yours yet to come, an echo of what you already know within your heart.

"Could it be that our dreams parallel one another and converge as we pass on to others the gift we have been given? The myths and adventures of previous ages come to life through living our own lives fully and deliberately. Our lives, too, become mythic as we experience the universal, timeless truths in our own way.

"To stumble once in a while is part of our journey. Taking that first step into the unknown enables us to find our greatest support, to learn that we are not alone, and that others before us have also walked our path. Every place you have been, every thought, worry, and fear you have ever had is already part of our collective experience.

"Confronting the unknown with courage reveals to us a capacity greater than we thought we had. Facing difficulty gives us greater confidence; experiencing success gives us a glimpse of what is to come. Even temptations contribute to our growth when we hold firmly to the values we have set for ourselves.

"Sooner or later along our path a deeper responsibility begins to stir within us, awakening a new desire to discover how fulfilling life can really be. This is your moment to arise, to give back the love you have been given."

After class, surprised by my own voice, I was confident that I could be honest with myself and also speak my truth to others. Through this experience, I have come to better understand my role in the teaching and learning process.

And I was beginning to feel like maybe I had found my direction, even my calling. I knew from my own experience now that I could welcome each moment as it came and be grateful for what it brought.

VISION

In the final minutes of the last class, after having become comfortable with each other and our deepest thoughts, I wanted to speak as clearly and openly as I could. "Early in my youth, I enjoyed many quiet walks on the beach beside these waters. Here, my inner purpose took root and grew within me.

"Dreams have a pulse of their own and seek their own attainment. In your heart is a vision waiting to come forth and guide you. It will unfold in its own time, slowly transforming your life into a miracle.

"We each walk a sacred path every day of our lives. Its holiness becomes clearer with each conscious step we take. Listen carefully to the silence of your own heart, and you will hear the sacred voice within you.

"We live in a time of engagement, not withdrawal. Fellowship and harmony are the brightest lights of a life well lived. Follow your own dream to a better world."

A student who rarely spoke asked, "How can you see a world filled with hope when we see despair all around us?"

At that moment, I was reminded what a privilege it was to be a teacher, to facilitate such an exchange of sincerity. I answered firmly, "The despair you see is real, yet it hides a world that is visible only when you look with the eyes of love and oneness. Hope and despair coexist and fuel each other always.

"All things in this physical realm change in time. The pain we see around us does not last forever. A dark night is but a brush stroke from the morning light. Even the journey of the soul has obstacles in its path. Be patient; everything that happens is all part of a sacred pattern of change and renewal.

"This pattern of birth, death, and rebirth is designed to bring about transformation, yet sometimes people get lost in the middle—or muddle—of the process, see nothing else, mistake this for their destiny, and feel stuck there. But time refuses to stand still and urges us on to complete the process.

"There are forces assisting us each step of the way. A sure sign that we are moving closer to our goal is when we sense that we are in a hopeless predicament, but at the last moment, some form of aid or guidance comes from an unexpected place, giving us the means to carry on, and it is then that we find a resolution to our muddle.

"The personal and the collective despair we see around us is transitory yet purposeful, like the muddles that come and go in our lives. They will take their course, here one moment and gone the next. Both happiness and sadness have their places in this world. But we needn't get caught up in either."

Another student asked, "Is this 'collective despair' the kind of thing McLuhan was warning us about with his idea of the 'global village'"?

"Great question!" I responded. "The global village we recognize more and more that we do live in certainly does have the potential to become a place where despair takes over. But our growing interdependence also has the potential to bring us socially, culturally, and even politically and spiritually closer together, too, as a world community. The technology turning the world into a village is but a neutral tool; we who use it can give it meaning and maybe a morality.

"The potential of this inherent tension has been with us forever. It was Socrates who said, twenty-five centuries ago, 'I am not an Athenian or a Greek but a citizen of the world.' Never has there been a time when this inclusive identity was more vital, or more possible, than this very moment. The world grows smaller with each day, with each thought of the whole. This deeper, fuller identity represents our greatest potential.

"The key to the direction we decide to go is already within us. Like a ray of light from the sun, our soul gives us our only changeless identity, the one that we are endowed with at conception, and which we carry with us throughout eternity.

"The soul identifies us as divine in essence and is what affords us the spiritual progress we make in this world. The soul's inclination is always toward the loftiest realm. It is guided solely by the power of love, which is the primary cause of the betterment of the world.

"Though we carry many other identities, we have but one essential identity that remains constant throughout this life and the next. Our spiritual nature is our core identity, the only identity that links us to all other human beings. Since we live in both the transitory and eternal realms at the same time, one of our greatest challenges is to keep our focus on the changeless essence within us and within everyone else.

"Piercing the veils of the seasons of life helps to give us a perspective of the whole. From our winters, we come to know our springs better. Embracing each season of life, remembering that the season of loss is followed by a season of harvest, will help us see all the seasons as phases of one interconnected whole.

"The soul is the meeting ground between the human and the divine. This life, because of its vicissitudes, its wonders *and* its despair, prepares us for the life to come. To experience the unseen in the seen is a true test of vision. Pain is not less than joy, or even separate from it. Each struggle we endure is essential to our growth and renewal. A time will come when we will see beyond duality to the oneness that brought everything into existence."

Another student looked puzzled. "Do you mean that the despair and pain we see are not important?" she asked.

"Everything has its place and purpose," I answered. "The dynamic tension between all things is necessary. Joy cannot exist without sorrow. Sorrow creates a yearning for its opposite. The two forces continually wrestle with each other, yet neither wins forever. The season of doubt is followed by the season of certainty. Yet even certainty is subject to the return of doubt; but this is what confirms us in our understanding of who we really are. When we know from our own experience that joy and sorrow can embrace each other, creating a greater unity, we have found the heart of life. Our ongoing effort to become more conscious of this inherent oneness is the greatest adventure we can set out on."

I paused for a moment. As I looked around the circle, all the students were listening, patiently waiting. So I concluded with my innermost thoughts.

"Many years ago, as a curious child, a voice came to me telling me that someday I would know God. I did not know what that meant then. I have since found that, even though we can never fully know God, the greatest pursuit of all is to seek the Unknowable.

"Revered in the myriad prayers, rituals, and sacred stories of all the diverse peoples, the Great Mystery, the Unseen, the Eternal, the Help in Peril, the Lord of all humanity, is known by a thousand names the world over. When we find a name expressing this Essence that appeals to our mind and touches our heart, we have found our connection to the one Spirit. More important than anything else is our conscious relationship with our Creator.

"The more we know of creation and its eternal principles, the more there is to know. Only through reflections of the Divine, such as the workings of nature and the words of the prophets, can we come closer to knowing Ultimate Reality.

"In seeking to know the Infinite, we come to know more of the grand design that is life. This is how we also come to better understand our own potential and our part in its unfolding.

"The only difference that matters in this life is the difference between the temporal and the everlasting. While all else around us is uncertain and inconsistent, only the Changeless remains constant and permanent. From the moonwalk comes a vision we all share, one of the clearest images of the Changeless: the heavens encircling the earth in a loving embrace. Remembering this often unites mind and soul, and one and all.

"We have all come from the same Source, and we are on a journey back to where we came from. The most sacred endeavors along our path are to love, to serve, and to remember. Could remembering where we have come from, who we are, what matters most in our life, and where we are going be our most vital spiritual practice?

"Sometimes it takes so little on our part to bring so much our way from the spiritual realm. And sometimes we expend so little in giving so much to others; yet this is how we become instruments of grace ourselves.

"The brightest light is the one that passes from heart to heart. As a wave of love washing over all on earth, this light is awakening us all to a time of promise, a moment of destiny. Evolution is the journey toward the recognition of the oneness of all and the holiness of everything.

"As we each move on, our thoughts of one another will grow into an echo of compassion; this is when we know we are never alone. Is the leaf, though it has its own branch, and its own call, ever not part of the tree? We, too, have grown together, as members of one human family, always part of the same sacred creation, and we shall remain part of each other as we continue on through the season of eternity. Our joy is in our lasting unity."

"In the Rose Garden of changeless splendor
a Flower hath begun to bloom,
compared to which
every other flower is but a thorn,
and before the brightness of Whose glory
the very essence of beauty
must pale and wither.
Arise, therefore, and,
with the whole enthusiasm of your hearts,
with all the eagerness of your souls,
the full fervor of your will,
and the concentrated efforts of your entire being,
strive to attain the paradise of His presence,
and endeavor to inhale the fragrance
of the incorruptible Flower,
to breathe the sweet savors of holiness,
and to obtain a portion of this perfume of celestial glory."
—Bahá'u'lláh, *Gleanings*, no. 151.3.

Notes & Afterthoughts

This section is meant primarily to bring the previously mentioned events into the present and to provide a few necessary endnotes. One thing I did not want the publication of this memoir to indicate is that I am living in the past. Nothing could be further from the case. However, as Schopenhauer might say, this time in my life has given me much of the text of my life while the next nearly forty years have supplied the commentary on it. I see this as a good thing since this formative time in my life did provide the meaning for almost everything else that has followed. A great deal has transpired since this time, but this pivotal period formed a firm foundation upon which the evolution of my life has taken place.

These formative events of my life have recently come full circle by connecting with certain thoughts and experiences of my present life that illustrate a deep continuity. A few recent events, which I will get to shortly, were not planned by me yet could not have been better timed. These afterthoughts can only point to a few of the main threads that still connect my life today with this earlier time. The threads of continuity between my past and present experiences have remained strong and are still prominent upon the surface of my life.

SUMMER

Margaret Fuller's pioneering feminist work (p. 18) is *Woman in the Nineteenth Century* (1845), edited by Donna Dickenson (Oxford: Oxford University Press, 1994).

FALL

Walt Whitman's inspired and visionary expression of the self in relation to the universe (pp. 52–54) is from "Song of Myself," *Leaves of Grass* (New York: Signet Classics, 2005).

William Blake's mystical juxtaposition of time and eternity (p. 54) is from "Auguries of Innocence" in *Poetry and Prose of William Blake*, edited by G. Keynes (New York: Viking, 1990).

C. G. Jung's inner-oriented autobiographical "personal myth" (pp. 54–55) is from *Memories, Dreams, Reflections* (New York: Vintage Books, 1989).

Henry David Thoreau's wise words on how and why to live in the present and in harmony with nature (p. 57) are from *Walden* (New York: Signet Classics, 2004).

Ralph Waldo Emerson's thoughts on the reliance of divine providence (pp. 57–58) are from "Self Reliance," in *The Portable Emerson*, edited by Carl Bode (New York: Penguin Classics, 1981).

Arlo Guthrie's song of his mystical experience, "Gabriel's Mother's Highway Ballad #16 Blues," (pp. 73–74) is found on his *Washington County* album. On the recorded version, he added the lines: "The sun come up while I wrote this song/Come on, children, come on/To remember me that it won't be long/Come on, children, come on."

WINTER

Joseph Campbell's pioneering work on comparative mythology describing the monomyth, or the pattern common to all the world's myths, *Hero with a Thousand Faces* (p. 80), was first published in 1949 by the Bollingen Foundation and is now a classic. My own book, *The Gift of Stories: Practical and Spiritual Applications of Autobiography, Life Stories and Personal Mythmaking* (Westport, CT: Greenwood Press, 1995), adapts the pattern of the monomyth to contemporary circumstances and settings for personal mythmaking.

Joseph Campbell's talk at Cooper Union (pp. 80–82), "Schizophrenia—the Inward Journey," is published as chapter 10 in *Myths to Live By* (New York: Viking Press, 1972).

The dream of the seven angels (pp. 94–99) is an allegorical illustration of how God reveals His Word over time through chosen prophets. Each angel represents one of the pure channels, or manifestations of the Divine, through which God communicates indirectly to us periodically throughout history. Each conveys the essence of a universal, timeless spiritual truth, each coming from the same source. We know them as the Prophets of God, or the founders of the world's great religions: Krishna, Moses, Zoroaster, Buddha, Christ, Muḥammad, and Bahá'u'lláh. They are the spiritual educators of humanity.

The Bible of the World (pp. 101–2), edited by Robert O. Ballou, was originally published by Viking Penguin in 1957 and is available now in a condensed form as *The Portable World Bible* (New York: Penguin, 1977).

The Religions of Man (pp. 102–3) by Huston Smith, first published by Harper & Row in 1958 and by Perennial Library in 1965, is now available as *The World's Religions: Our Great Wisdom Traditions* (San Francisco: HarperSanFrancisco, 1991).

The brochure I picked up at a sloop festival (pp. 104–5) was my first introduction to the Bahá'í Faith. The concept of "progressive revelation," which it explained, seemed natural to me; it made intuitive sense immediately. The idea is that one God created one people with one continuously unfolding system of religion designed to shed more and more light upon the creation. The same essential spiritual truths are revealed at different times in different places by different prophets, all of whom are bearers of the same essential message. As differences and variants appear, and as each cycle of revelation wanes, another is begun. In every age, a fresh voice renews the changeless word of God. The essence of all the Prophets of God is the same. They understand their own unity as well as their common purpose: to guide humanity from the darkness of ignorance to the light of true understanding and to ensure the peace and tranquillity of mankind. Each is as a divine physician offering a remedy for the well-being of humanity. Bahá'-u'lláh, in our time, has reestablished the quintessence of the teachings of all the prophets.

This conscious recognition of the nature of progressive revelation intensified my search for common themes, principles, motifs, and archetypes in the world's religions. It was about three years later that I first came into contact with Bahá'ís. I was living in Spartanburg, South Carolina, and had become friends with a few Bahá'ís around my age. Many things struck me about them as individuals: their insightfulness, their clarity about religious and spiritual issues, their holistic perspective, and their conviction in what they believed. I was especially impressed by their commitment to a personal and collective spiritual life. One Bahá'í also particularly impressed me with her recitation of Bahá'í prayers from memory. When I spoke with another about my interests in mythology and mysticism, he said he thought I would also be interested in reading Bahá'u'lláh's mystical work known as the Seven Valleys. He was right.

This was the first Bahá'í book I read, and it convinced me that Bahá'u'lláh had a much deeper, divinely inspired insight into not only the pattern itself but also its purpose for our spiritual development. The poetic, allegorical language captured the universality of the stages of the journey of the soul like nothing else had for me, having been familiar with the essential pattern of this journey from the work of both Joseph Campbell and Evelyn Underhill, especially her classic *Mysticism* (New York: E. P. Dutton, 1961). I then read more from the Bahá'í writings on other topics that intrigued me, including the history of the Bahá'í Faith, and its sorely needed spiritual principles, which also felt intuitive to me, especially in the time in which we live. I soon became a Bahá'í and began to incorporate the principles and teachings of the Bahá'í Faith into my daily spiritual life.

I would suggest, for further reading—in addition to the books described in the end pages here, especially if you have areas of interest similar to mine—*Bahá'u'lláh and the New Era* (Wilmette, IL: Bahá'í Publishing, 2006) and *The Bahá'í Faith: The Emerging Global Religion* (Wilmette, IL: Bahá'í Publishing, 2002) as excellent overall general introductions, in addition to *The Seven Valleys and The Four Valleys* (Wilmette, IL: Bahá'í Publishing Trust, 1991), *Gleanings from the Writings of Bahá'u'lláh* (Wilmette, IL: Bahá'í Publishing, 2005), and *The Hidden Words* (Wilmette, IL: Bahá'í Publishing, 2002). These books reveal the essence of the writings of Bahá'u'lláh, especially on the topics of God's love for humanity, our relationship with God, and the nature, purpose, and outcome of life. *Some Answered Questions* (Wilmette, IL: Bahá'í Publishing Trust, 1984) and *The Promulgation of Universal Peace* (Wilmette, IL: Bahá'í Publishing Trust, 2008) from the writings of 'Abdu'l-Bahá, address issues of spiritual development and the principles underlying the Bahá'í Faith.

Another way to approach the writings of Bahá'u'lláh and 'Abdu'l-Bahá is through the excellent topical compilations *The Divine Art of Living* (Wilmette, IL: Bahá'í Publishing, 2006), which addresses learning to know and love God, faith and certitude, detachment and sacrifice, obedience and humility, tests and ordeals, health and healing, marriage and family life, and peace and unity; and *The Reality of Man* (Wilmette, IL: Bahá'í Publishing, 2005), which discusses our spiritual reality, the nature of the soul, immortality and life hereafter, and the divine educators. Also useful is *Bahá'u'- lláh's Teachings on Spiritual Reality* (Riviera Beach, FL: Palabra Publications, 1996), which focuses on the quest for spirituality, the spiritual life, material and spiritual reality, the progress of the soul, and humanity's spiritual education.

SPRING

It was when I spoke with Joseph Campbell in more depth in his home in Greenwich Village (pp. 111–12) that I became even more aware of the contemporary role of the ageless motifs and archetypes in our lives today. Linking more directly and specifically my own archetypal experiences to the pattern of the monomyth, and thinking of the process of the adventure that he described as departure-initiation-return in terms of beginning-muddle-resolution, enabled me to develop a contemporary version of this ageless pattern that could be applied to our own experiences today. This is what became chapter 5, "Universalizing Your Story: Personal Mythmaking," and chapter 6, "Merging Your Personal Myth with the Collective Myth," in my book, *The Gift of Stories*.

Plato's allegory of the cave (pp. 114–15), a great lesson in going beyond the obvious, can be found in *The Republic* (New York: Penguin Classics, 2003).

Confucius' "The Great Learning" (p. 115), illustrating the virtues of humility and harmony, is found in *Confucian*

Analects, The Great Learning, & The Doctrine of the Mean, translated, with notes, by James Legge, Dover Publications.

Emerson's emphasis on the importance of the influence of nature on learning and creativity in "The American Scholar" (pp. 115–17) can be found in *The Portable Emerson,* edited by Carl Bode.

Black Elk's vision (p. 117), which consisted of hearing a sacred voice and coming to an understanding of his purpose in life, is in *Black Elk Speaks,* by John G. Neihardt (New York: Pocket Books, 1972).

Arlo Guthrie's "Highway in the Wind" (p. 121), used by permission of Appleseed Music, is on his *Alice's Restaurant* album.

Walt Whitman's "Song of the Open Road" (p. 122) comes from his poem "Song of Myself."

Laura Nyro's "Time and Love" (pp. 123–24) is used by permission of EMI/Blackwood Music and is on her album of the same title.

The Moody Blues' "The Balance," written by Graeme Edge, (pp. 125–26) is used by permission of Threshold Music and is on the album *Question of Balance.*

The course on folk-rock lyrics as poetry was the first college course I taught (pp. 119–35) and the only time I taught that particular course. It was in many ways a unique, even magical, experience. Not all of my teaching since then has been as smooth, as confirming, or as rewarding. I have in fact had many classes that have included struggle along with the "shining moments," as they are called. There are bound to be those few who just do not relate to what I try to do, at least in part because I teach not as much to pass on information about a content area out there but to help others discover more of their own inner truth.

The ongoing effort to connect with as many of my students as possible is a regular challenge, as is remembering to let my gratitude for all that has come my way be evident, somehow, in all that I do. To have been given the opportunity to live the questions of my life, and to be able to speak of them, heart-to-heart with others, is my greatest blessing.

Without a doubt, the most important learning I received from my series of experiences of 1969, and what has been the single most sustaining aspect in all my efforts since then, in the way I approach my teaching as well as living my own life, has been an unfailing hope for the future, an undying hope for humanity. The awareness I came to then has given me a perspective on the world that cannot be changed, no matter what, or how much, changes around me.

Two recent classroom moments have brought my teaching and learning experiences full circle, and right back to the closeness and honesty I felt from the discussions we had in the first college class I ever taught. At the end of the spring 2007 semester graduate course in human development, we were considering non-Western classics, one of which was the Seven Valleys, by Bahá'u'lláh. I was identifying some of the motifs of transformation that appear in this poetic, mystical expression of the stages of human development and how they compare to the motifs and archetypes found in Joseph Campbell's *Hero with a Thousand Faces*. We had earlier in the course covered my contemporary version of this in *The Gift of Stories* that I had called the story model of adult development (beginning, muddle, resolution). I noted in particular the motif appearing in the Valley of Search: "At every step, aid from the Invisible Realm will attend him and the heat of his search will grow." I compared this to the motif of "supernatural aid" coming during the Departure phase of Campbell's monomyth.

Then a student spoke up and said, "That seems so airy. I don't get how that can relate to real life at all."

After a thoughtful moment of silence, I said, "Maybe an example from my own life might help," and I told the story of how I was led to Joseph Campbell's *Hero with a Thousand Faces* for the first time while being drawn into a bookstore and then noticing a poster announcing his talk that evening a few blocks away, which I then attended (pp. 80–82). I pointed out that the important part to that assistance coming to me was how I chose to respond to it. I also happened to mention that this experience is part of my memoir of 1969 that describes a transformative time in my life.

A couple of weeks later, I read in this students' course journal, as the last paragraph of the final reflection on the course as a whole, "I really enjoyed Dr. Atkinson's self-disclosing story in our second-to-last class. It was nice to hear a personal story, and it made me realize that 'The Seven Valleys' is not as 'out there' as I had thought. I appreciated his openness to share with us and look forward to his book coming out next year."

The second moment also occurred at the end of the spring 2007 semester in my graduate course "Culture, Tradition, and Diversity." In the final class, as a way to wrap up our discussions on diversity, ethnicity, and multiple identities, I passed around a drawing from Guy Murchie's *The Seven Mysteries of Life* (New York: Mariner Books, 1999, ch. 13) that illustrated the interrelatedness of the human family. It consisted of a "you" at the center surrounded by all the relatives we could ever have—parents, aunts, uncles, grandparents, and cousins, all extending outward from the center with arrows connecting everyone. The drawing made it clear that, depending on how far back we go, we have over a thousand fifth cousins, over a million tenth cousins, and that every other person on this planet (of any ethnicity) is at least in the range of fiftieth cousin, making us all one human family.

I connected this to the role of counselors, educators, and other professionals in bringing about a greater awareness of the fact that we are one family. I said, "I believe that humanity will eventually become aware of its relatedness. As we've seen in this course, there are more and more scientific affirmations of this all the time. We may not see the full awareness of this in our lifetimes, but sometime in the future this understanding will be as clear to our descendants as our relationship to our 'blood' relatives is to us today. And this will change the way we relate to and behave towards each other."

Then a student asked, "Have you always been so optimistic?"

I reflected for a moment and said, *"Always* is a long time. I don't think children are really ready to always be optimistic. Most adolescents are probably not, either. But there comes a time in our lives when certain kinds of experiences, combined with a maturity of thought, make it possible for us to always be optimistic if we choose to be. There was a time in my life when I became conscious of certain things that gave me an understanding of where our collective evolution is leading us, even though there are times that feel like we are going backwards."

I mentioned that I was referring to the time in my life when I first came to the conscious awareness of—and belief in—the oneness of humanity, that nothing could ever change my mind enough again to cause me to go back to a previous way of viewing the world, and that this really does change forever the way I see and relate to others.

This abiding sense of hope was first given to me in my experiences of 1969 and confirmed in my reading of Bahá'u'lláh's Seven Valleys and in every other aspect of the Bahá'í writings. In describing the journey of the soul, Bahá'u'lláh says that, in order for anyone to move beyond the Valley of Search, we need patience, that we should never be downhearted, that we should not falter, and He reminds us that we will be guided and aided at every step. Then, in the Valley of Love, where reason is burned to ashes, we find that we cannot distinguish guidance from error. But this is a necessary step that leads us further on to the Valley of Knowledge, where we come out of doubt and into certitude, as our inner eyes are opened, and the doors of vain imaginings are shut, as we recognize providence in all things. The journey of the soul continues through the remaining valleys, where we grow to look on all things with the eye of oneness, becoming content, knowing wonderment in all things, and living in the richness of the spiritual world. The Bahá'í principles and teachings as a whole provide the basis for this much-needed hope and assurance.

Obviously, the world has continued to change dramatically over the last four decades, and in ways that do not always seem for the better. Yet this core awareness of our oneness also gives us a vantage point from where we can recognize that a lifetime is but a moment in eternity, that our lives are links in an endless chain, connecting us to those who have come before us and to those who will come after us, and that what we each do in our lives contributes something to the next moment in eternity.

One other recent event has brought my adventures of 1969 full circle. In late May of 2007, I realized the fulfillment of the end of my dream at the monastery (pp. 94–99) on my Bahá'í pilgrimage to the Holy Land. Upon this hallowed ground, in the city of Acre, Israel, and on nearby Mt. Carmel, I walked in the footsteps of the prophets of God, experiencing directly a spiritual heritage common to all. A pilgrimage to Israel, a unique spiritual journey in itself, confirmed the reality of the concept of evolution in religion.

I approached this pilgrimage, a gift beyond all others, with humbleness and devotion. Pilgrimage is indeed a mystical dream if we could but see all that we encounter with the eyes of the earliest pilgrims. I sought to envision the essence of what they may have seen, to meditate in the tranquillity of these holy precincts in order to listen and absorb as much as was possible, that I too might be inspired.

Our group of over two hundred pilgrims from all parts of the world circumambulated the golden-domed Shrine of the Báb in silent prayer. On the same level as this majestic edifice, and extending outward above it and below it, are nineteen beautifully landscaped terraces, a heavenly path from the mountaintop to the city of Haifa below.

Surrounded by exquisite gardens, this blessed spot is set apart from all others with verdant trees and plants, colorful flowers of sweet scents, and fountains of flowing water. This vision of paradise exists solely for the praise of the Divine; its beauty and magnificence is a symbol of the transformation that the hearts of humanity, and even the entire world, will someday undergo.

In the mansion of Bahjí, in the room where Bahá'u'lláh lived during the final years of His life, I reflected with deepest reverence upon the words used in 1890 by the distinguished University of Cambridge scholar Edward G. Browne to record his impressions of his meeting with Bahá'u'lláh: "In the corner where the divan met the wall sat a wondrous and venerable figure. . . . The face of him on whom I gazed I can never forget, though I cannot describe it. Those piercing eyes seemed to read one's very soul; power and authority sat on that ample brow. . . . No need to ask in whose presence I stood, as I bowed myself before one who is the object of a devotion and love which kings might envy and emperors sigh for in vain!"*

Another day, sitting alone in the Shrine of 'Abdu'l-Bahá, for a brief but timeless moment—one to carry with me through all eternity—deep in meditation, I became lost in the remembrance of God.

---

* E. G. Browne, introduction to *A Traveler's Narrative,* as quoted in *Bahá'u'lláh and the New Era* (Wilmette, IL: Bahá'í Publishing, 2006), p. 46.

And in the prison cell where Bahá'u'lláh and others suffered such deprivation and indignity, I heard only words of comfort and confirmation: Your dream is real. Time is an illusion. Humanity *is* one, in all the worlds of God.

In the Shrine of Bahá'u'lláh, with a revivifying breeze blowing over me, overwhelmed by the undeniable spirit of holiness, my heart was moved with a tenderness never before known, and my deepest prayer flowed forth.

And in the faces of my fellow pilgrims, I beheld an inner joy, instilled by the precious bounty we all shared, even though it might be more than a lifetime before we would fully appreciate its significance for us. We all shared, as well, that which we each treasured most—the advent of divine justice, the unity and prosperity of humankind, and the promise of world peace.

*"More than ever today when the world
is facing such a crisis of bewilderment and unrest,
must we stand firm in faith
seeking that which binds together
instead of tearing apart.
To those searching for light,
the Bahá'í Teachings offer a star
which will lead them to deeper understanding,
to assurance, peace, and good will with all men."*
—Queen Marie of Romania, 1936

A Basic Bahá'í Reading List

The following list provides a sampling of works conveying the spiritual truths, social principles, and history of the Bahá'í Faith.

INTRODUCTORY WORKS

Bahá'í International Community, Office of Public Information, New York. *Bahá'u'lláh*. Wilmette, IL: Bahá'í Publishing Trust, 1991.

Bowers, Kenneth E. *God Speaks Again: An Introduction to the Bahá'í Faith*. Wilmette, IL: Bahá'í Publishing, 2004.

Hatcher, William S., and J. Douglas Martin. *The Bahá'í Faith: The Emerging Global Religion*. Wilmette, IL: Bahá'í Publishing, 2002.

Smith, Peter. *A Concise Encyclopedia of the Bahá'í Faith*. Oxford: Oneworld Publications, 2000.

SELECTED WRITINGS OF BAHÁ'U'LLÁH

Gleanings from the Writings of Bahá'u'lláh. Translated by Shoghi Effendi. Wilmette, IL: Bahá'í Publishing, 2005.

The Hidden Words. Translated by Shoghi Effendi. Wilmette, IL: Bahá'í Publishing, 2002.

The Kitáb-i-Aqdas: The Most Holy Book. Wilmette, IL: Bahá'í Publishing Trust, 1993.

The Kitáb-i-Íqán: The Book of Certitude. Translated by Shoghi Effendi. Wilmette, IL: Bahá'í Publishing, 2003.

Tablets of Bahá'u'lláh revealed after the Kitáb-i-Aqdas. Compiled by the Research Department of the Universal House of Justice. Translated by Habib Taherzadeh. 1st ps ed. Wilmette, IL: Bahá'í Publishing Trust, 1998.

SELECTED WRITINGS OF 'ABDU'L-BAHÁ

Paris Talks: Addresses given by 'Abdu'l-Bahá in Paris in 1911. Wilmette, IL: Bahá'í Publishing, 2006.

The Promulgation of Universal Peace: Talks Delivered by 'Abdu'l-Bahá during His Visit to the United States and Canada in 1912. Compiled by Howard MacNutt. 2nd ed. Wilmette, IL: Bahá'í Publishing Trust, 1982.

The Secret of Divine Civilization. Translated by Marzieh Gail and Ali-Kuli Khán. Wilmette, IL: Bahá'í Publishing, 2007.

Selections from the Writings of 'Abdu'l-Bahá. Compiled by the Research Department of the Universal House of Justice. Translated by a Committee at the Bahá'í World Center and Marzieh Gail. Wilmette, IL: Bahá'í Publishing Trust, 1997.

Some Answered Questions. Compiled and translated by Laura Clifford Barney. 1st ps ed. Wilmette, IL: Bahá'í Publishing Trust, 1984.

Index

The *Clearwater* is a 106-foot wooden sailing sloop designed after eighteenth- and nineteenth-century Dutch sailing sloops. In 1966, folksinger and activist Pete Seeger had the vision that the public would come to care for all of our threatened waterways by learning to care for one boat and one river. He inspired a group of dedicated people who made the dream a reality. Launched in 1969, the *Clearwater* serves as a moveable classroom, laboratory, stage, and forum. More than a dozen national and international programs have successfully modeled programs after those pioneered by the *Clearwater*.

Each year, the *Clearwater* accommodates nearly thirteen thousand children and adults for educational excursions that teach history, biology, and environmental science and navigation along the Hudson River, New York Harbor, and Long Island Sound. Thousands more are reached through on-land classroom visits, field programs, and public exhibits.

For more information, visit www.clearwater.org.

Bahá'í
PUBLISHING
and the BAHÁ'Í FAITH

Bahá'í Publishing produces books based on the teachings of the Bahá'í Faith. Founded over 160 years ago, the Bahá'í Faith has spread to some 235 nations and territories and is now accepted by more than five million people. The word "Bahá'í" means "follower of Bahá'u'lláh." Bahá'u'lláh, the founder of the Bahá'í Faith, asserted that he is the Messenger of God for all of humanity in this day. The cornerstone of his teachings is the establishment of the spiritual unity of human-kind, which will be achieved by personal transformation and the ap-plication of clearly identified spiritual principles. Bahá'ís also believe that there is but one religion and that all the Messengers of God—among them Abraham, Zoroaster, Moses, Krishna, Buddha, Jesus, and Muḥammad—have progressively revealed its nature. Together, the world's great religions are expressions of a single, unfolding divine plan. Human beings, not God's Messengers, are the source of reli-gious divisions, prejudices, and hatreds.

The Bahá'í Faith is not a sect or denomination of another religion, nor is it a cult or a social movement. Rather, it is a globally recognized independent world religion founded on new books of scripture re-vealed by Bahá'u'lláh.

Bahá'í Publishing is an imprint of the National Spiritual Assembly of the Bahá'ís of the United States.

For more information about the Bahá'í Faith,
or to contact Bahá'ís near you, visit
http://www.bahai.us/
or call
1-800-22-UNITE

OTHER BOOKS AVAILABLE FROM
BAHÁ'Í PUBLISHING

MEDITATIONS
Selections from Bahá'í Scripture
edited by Bahá'í Publishing
$19.00 U.S. / $21.00 CAN
Trade paper
ISBN-10: 1-931847-56-8
ISBN-13: 978-1-931847-56-8

Meditations is a collection of passages that helps to encourage and support the habit of regular reflection and meditation and assists readers of any faith on their spiritual path. A rich and inspiring sample of the vast body of Bahá'í scripture, this collection will appeal to everyone. It includes passages from the writings of Bahá'u'lláh, as well as from those of His forerunner, the Báb, and those of His son 'Abdu'l-Bahá.

Among the teachings of Bahá'u'lláh is that the primary purpose of life is to know and to love God. In the Bahá'í Faith, as in every religion, prayer and meditation are fundamental tools for spiritual development. Their daily practice enables us to commune with God and sustains and strengthens our souls. Through daily meditation, Bahá'u'lláh writes, "the secret of things unseen" is revealed and "the sweetness of a spiritual and imperishable fragrance" is inhaled.

FROM A GNAT TO AN EAGLE
The Story of Nathan Rutstein
by Nathan Rutstein
$18.00 U.S. / $20.00 CAN
Trade paper
ISBN-10: 1-931847-46-0
ISBN-13: 978-1-931847-46-9

From a Gnat to an Eagle is the story of Nathan Rutstein's life in his own humble words, a story of spiritual transformation and personal triumph.

The child of Jewish immigrants living in the Bronx, Nathan Rutstein was raised in a home devoid of books and ran the streets with gangs as a youth. When he was admitted to college on a sports scholarship, he seemed headed for a career in baseball, but the pursuit of justice—particularly racial equality—motivated him to apply himself to his studies and aim for something nobler.

Unaware at first of his own spiritual nature, Nathan emerged from his youth with a deep thirst for personal spiritual growth rooted in the teachings of the Bahá'í Faith. Though nothing in his upbringing encouraged him to pursue the life of the mind, eventually he became an author, a teacher, and a tireless advocate for racial equality, which became the dominating passion of his life. The book is a compelling account of a remarkable man and an illuminating portrait of how a person can be transformed through the power of love, dedication, and perseverance in the path of personal spiritual development.

ILLUMINE MY HEART
Bahá'í Prayers for Every Occasion
by Bahá'u'lláh, the Báb, and 'Abdu'l-Bahá
$12.00 U.S. /$13.50 CAN
Trade paper
ISBN-10: 1-931847-53-3
ISBN-13: 978-1-931847-53-7

Illumine My Heart is a collection of prayers from the sacred writings of the Bahá'í Faith. The prayers included here will assist spiritual seekers to walk a spiritual path with practical feet and to navigate the ups and downs of life with comfort and assurance. There are prayers that deal with the tests and difficulties we face in everyday life, prayers for healing and bereavement, prayers we can say for loved ones who have passed away, prayers for families and marriage, for young children, and for peace and unity. In *Illumine My Heart,* readers will find a wellspring of soul-stirring and uplifting words to accompany them on every stage of life's journey.

WAITING FOR THE SUNRISE
One Family's Struggle against Genocide and Racism
by Elizabeth Gatorano
$19.00 U.S. / $21.00 CAN
Trade paper
ISBN-10: 1-931847-45-2
ISBN-13: 978-1-931847-45-2

Waiting for the Sunrise is the personal account of an interracial family's struggle against pervasive racism in the U.S. and the horrors of the civil war that plagued Rwanda in 1994. Raised in the American Midwest, author Elizabeth Gatorano, who is White, had no idea of the trials she would face after marrying Phanuel, who is Black and an immigrant to the U.S. from Rwanda. Prejudice against their marriage followed them and their children wherever they went, often making them the focus of racist discrimination and threats of violence at home and at work.

In 1994, when fighting broke out in Rwanda, both Liz and Phanuel worked diligently to bring as many members of his family to safety as they could. Yet the harrowing rescue of his family from Rwanda was only the beginning of the difficult journey that lay ahead. Faced with the challenges of adapting to a new culture in a foreign country, Phanuel's family struggled to adjust to life in the U.S. The relatives' gratitude gradually gave way to the fears and prejudices they brought with them from Rwanda, and Liz and Phanuel eventually found themselves the targets of suspicion and hate from the very people they had helped to save.

Throughout these ordeals, Liz and Phanuel responded to hostility with love and patience, their faith in each other and in God remaining unshakable, even in the darkest hours. After accepting the Bahá'í Faith, they became even more committed to helping the less fortunate and personifying the virtues of love and unity found in the writings of Bahá'u'lláh. Together, they overcame all obstacles in their path, and they continue to help those in need today.

To view our complete catalog,
please visit http:// books.bahai.us